CW00556515

11/25

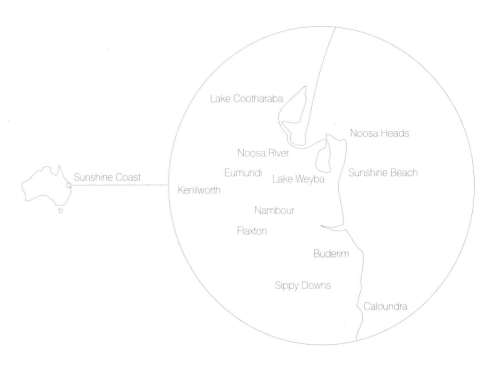

Sunshine Coast

Lake Cootharaba

Noosa Heads

Noosa River

Eumundi   Lake Weyba   Sunshine Beach

Kenilworth

Nambour

Flaxton

Buderim

Sippy Downs

Caloundra

LOCAL

Gabriel **Poole**
John **Mainwaring**
Lindsay and Kerry **Clare**

HEROES

Architects of Australia's Sunshine Coast

Text and Photography by Peter Hyatt
Foreword by Sir Zelman Cowen
Introduction by James Grose

CRAFTSMAN HOUSE

Contents

Preface
Peter Hyatt

For Jenny, Ella, Sunday and Ruby

While the architects in this book enjoy
their extended moment in the sun,
there are a few people who have helped
to bring the planets into alignment and
crystallise the process of publication.
Nevill Drury, publishing director of
Craftsman House, had the prescience
and energy to support this project with
minimal prodding. Steven Cornwell
is a graphic designer whose modernity is
hallmarked by such elegance as to seduce
the eye with seemingly effortless simplicity.
All four architects — Gabriel, John,
Kerry and Lindsay — have been
generous in the most unexpected ways,
which perhaps reflects the longevity
of our association and friendship.
Tammy Hromis of Carter Holt Harvey
and Catherine Johnston of James Hardie
have made a generous contribution by way
of sponsorship from built to published work.
Both companies' products are imaginatively
utilised by the architectural practices featured.
Finally, my partner Jennifer, whose original
idea it was to produce this book, has played
a capable midwife throughout the conception
and delivery of text and images. All are partners
in this project to recognise great talent.
They all deserve the extended therapy
of salt air and its buttered, late afternoon
light so evocative of the Sunshine Coast.

Foreword
Rt Hon. Sir Zelman Cowen
AK GCMG GCVO DCL

Australians have developed a tremendous confidence in sport, music and art, yet somehow this has never been replicated in our urban architecture. On the Sunshine Coast of all places, we find this design of great optimism and identity."

When I was Governor General, the Royal Australian Institute of Architects proposed that its major national award for public building be named after me. I readily agreed to this honour. It gave me great pleasure because the domestic architecture award is named after the late Robin Boyd with whom I had a cherished friendship.

In 1998 I was invited to take part in the ceremonial opening of the Sunshine Coast University Campus Library. It is a wonderfully elegant building which brings architectural distinction to the campus and provides an impressive central element. It is the creation of the Sunshine Coast architect John Mainwaring and Lawrence Nield of Sydney. Within one week of opening this building, I was invited to make the presentation of the national awards in the category of public and institutional buildings. It was with great pleasure that I announced the name John Mainwaring as architect of the library and made a presentation to him.

John Mainwaring's work, together with that of Gabriel Poole and Lindsay and Kerry Clare, is presented in this handsome book, *Local Heroes — Architects of Australia's Sunshine Coast*. They have chosen to practise in one of Australia's loveliest environments. I write with some feeling about this because, for many years, the Sunshine Coast has been my second home. When I came with my family to live and work in Brisbane in 1970, we enjoyed a simple cottage at Caloundra. It has given untold pleasure and repose for many years. It is not hard to see why the architects whose work is celebrated in this book should have chosen to practise in this environment.

Peter Hyatt has produced a vigorous and stimulating text. He tells of an earlier time twenty-five years ago, when Gabriel Poole employed Lindsay and Kerry Clare and, later, John Mainwaring. They have since gone their own ways but remained true to the principles of developing architecture of a unique and appropriate regional character. The decision to remain on the coast has meant they have depended on residential and small-scale public and commercial buildings and in this way made their distinctive contribution to architecture. Australians have developed a tremendous confidence in sport, music and art, yet somehow this has never been replicated in our urban architecture. On the Sunshine Coast of all places, we find this design of great optimism and identity.

The arrival of the University to the Sunshine Coast has presented new opportunities. John Mainwaring's library and the Clares' adjacent sports and recreation building show how well they have responded to the opportunity. These architects are winners of Australia's highest honour for residential design — the Robin Boyd Award. Between them they have won more than fifty state and national awards, and in 1998 Gabriel Poole was awarded the RAIA Gold Medal.

As one who has had a long association with architects, I welcome this book. It draws attention to great talents which exist in our nation. It effectively makes the point that the quality of the built environment is of profound importance.

Introduction
James Grose

The problem
with seeing
Clare/Mainwaring/
Poole buildings
is that
you expect
the entire
Sunshine Coast
– no, the entire
northern climes
– to be built
just like them.
Of course, the
Sunshine Coast
is as disappointing,
mediocre
and unrelenting
as any developer's
Nirvana, Tuscany,
Baltic Coast,
rural England
or Kyoto.

They're all available on a sliding scale of consumer expectation; on a sliding scale of architectural dread.

Why can't it be like architects want it to be? Too great a question. The important thing is that at least we have the joy of these three architects' work to punctuate, however minimally, the drabness of our coastal developments. Beyond that, their influence on Australian architecture is now becoming evident.

Gabriel Poole is an enigmatic figure, and his buildings do nothing to really define him. From his early buildings, to the Tent House and, most recently, his own house at Lake Weyba, his work is perhaps the most eclectic of the three. Certainly, it sits somewhere between 'building systems' and the temporal. The Quadropod houses developed a means of building on typical sloping coastal sites in the genre of Archigram's instant city of the 1960s. Unfortunately, a masonry-anchored development industry was unable to see the constructional benefit of such a system — let alone the relationship with the ground, the culture of the stilt Queensland house, the climatic response, the external imperative of hot-climate building, the architectural character and form — all of these unarguably derived from the experience of living on the Sunshine Coast.

At the Venice Biennale in 1991, I watched as Europeans were drawn to the celebratory imagery of the Tent House. Such a romantic relationship with the land is implausible in Europe. I saw their delight in the ephemeral quality of the tent — its flags, its very lightness and its obscure sense of humour.

John Mainwaring's buildings have a different sense of humour, a more larrikin, more self-effacing humour. Together with Lawrence Nield and Partners at the Sunshine Coast University Library, he has redefined campus architecture in Australia forever. None of the internal Eurocentric pondering of recent Melbourne campus buildings here — rather, simple engagement with place. But more importantly, an engagement with a generation and its attitude towards the new millennium. This is a building about democracy, about egalitarianism — it fundamentally speaks of a place and people that is energised and discovering itself.

If Mainwaring's buildings are leaping across the countryside, Lindsay and Kerry Clare's buildings sit quietly and calmly on the landscape. Much has been written of the Clares' work; the calm manipulation of light, the clarity of the plan and the Aalto lineage. It is this peaceful quality to the Clares' work that differentiates it from the current somewhat frenetic development of sticks and slats architecture of Queensland. It is subtle, sophisticated and timeless.

Mainwaring and the Clares met in Gabriel's practice and Gabriel is spoken of by all three as a mentor, as a father figure and as an architect who found expression in the early remoteness of the sandhills of the Sunshine Coast. Scattered throughout the region are buildings by other architects that are a clear testament to the influence of these three practices. Together with other Queensland architects, Peter O'Gorman and Brit Andresen, Donovan and Hill, Elizabeth Watson-Brown, John Hockings and others, a legitimate and defining language of architecture is emerging.

This is not just an architecture of climate, or a response to the materiality of the Queensland vernacular. It is an engagement with an emerging narrative that is at last defining the cultural realm of an Australian community. It is neither trite, clichéd nor simplistic, but rooted in the maturation of a country coming to grips with its difference.

For some time, this architecture has been discussed and examined in great detail in Australia's architectural journals and in *BHP Profile* in particular. Its editor and photographer Peter Hyatt has made a significant contribution. He has been unrelenting in his support and enthusiasm. *Local Heroes — Architects of Australia's Sunshine Coast* is further testament to his valuable contribution to the recording of this emerging Australian architecture.

Coastal bush near Little Cove provides a silhouetted iconography that informs and inspires the Sunshine Coast Group.

Local Heroes
Peter Hyatt

"… in the context of the open tenderness and authenticity of Jefferson's architecture, the very sophistication of Stanford's buildings exposes a kind of emptiness — as if the buildings were a performance, a kind of dressing-up; a charade. In Jefferson's architecture, in contrast, there is thoughtfulness, humility, love and above all conviction."

Suzannah Lessard
The Architect of Desire, Orion Books Ltd, London, 1997
a division of Weidenfeld & Nicolson Publishers (UK) and Dell Publishing (US)

There is an inevitability about some architecture that has nothing to do with wit, irony or 'isms' and absolutely everything to do with a connection between people and places. The monument is not alone in creating awe. The flawed aspiration deserves more applause than the immaculate dud. Unfortunately and so often, this is not the reality. A single jewel can easily outweigh the crown's competing clutter. Real architecture exposes virtuosity in the most unexpected of ways. It seduces the brain as well as the eye, is passionate and informed. It is restless in its pursuit of harmony and appropriate risk. It regards the smallest details as valuable behavioural traits to become the strands and nuances of personality. So much for the ideal. What we have instead is so much architecture of ignorance. No amount of money heaped on the modern city building seems to address the failed relationship at pavement level and blunt penetration of sky.

The mystique, if not sheer power, of skyscrapers has all but evaporated. In the 1990s the capacity for wonder has been dwarfed by facsimile and repetition. The past few decades in architecture mirror the crisis of modern art. Great work is in desperately short supply. Our cities and suburbs are thin on art but pumped with artifice. In this regard, we are all diminished because we are no longer partners in an adventure but prisoners to artificiality.

Architects have allowed accountants and investment managers to take charge of the design of our cities and suburbs. Short-sightedness flows from short-term investments. The spirituality of the church and shrine, with their spires and intricate craftsmanship, has fallen from popular grace. Architects have been elbowed out of calculations to a role of little more than exterior decorator. At the dawn of the new millennium, the profession remains challenged to produce work less driven by rhetoric, flattering graphics, the virtual worlds of super-computers and CAD. What it urgently needs is less RAM and much more damn. But there is also spectacular hope. This bankruptcy of ideas is fragmented and challenged by the confluence of special individuals and circumstance. It is at these fragile intersections of chance that the drama of

personalities and forces compress to convert coal into diamonds. It gives us the condensed, magisterial power of Norman Foster's Hongkong & Shanghai Bank and the coiled rhythms of Glenn Murcutt's pavilion at Binji Binji on the New South Wales south coast. It gives us fragments of cities and suburbs of delicate substance that pulsate like distant stars.

Australia's Sunshine Coast happens to be blessed with at least three architectural practices that are making a crucial difference. Situated on the central east coast of Queensland, occupying a small, subtropical patch just north of Brisbane, the region is rapidly coming into focus for many of the right reasons. This narrow, fragile coastal strip measuring around 200 kilometres long by 30 kilometres wide — edged by the Blackall Ranges to the west and the Pacific Ocean to the east — is the springboard for design which dramatically outperforms its provincial status. Three decades of work by this nucleus of modern architects is making its mark. That this phenomenon should occur at all is part fluke and part circumstance.

It has occurred, of course, for precisely the same reasons that special buildings occur — the intersection of forces and the confluence of special individuals. None of these things is inevitable. They struggle like saplings straining towards the sun but can be so easily cut down before becoming specimens. There is much to be said for loving what you do and the place where you work. The architecture of Gabriel Poole, John Mainwaring, and Lindsay and Kerry Clare reflects this attitude. Theirs is a statement about managing resources, handling materials and space, light and shade. A spirituality emerges from this, something few architects can claim.

It retains an innocence only made possible by astute observation; a feathered edge no less remarkable than a bird's wing, a slender strut seemingly borrowed from the wing of a dragonfly. This is the language of parts evolved that, in so much of their work, creates ease, animation and tension.

Below left A Pacific Rim influence is evident in Gabriel Poole's Hastings Street development (1984).
Opposite View north-west from Noosa Heads along Main Beach towards the Noosa River. In the distance is Cooloola National Park and beyond a sugarcane burnoff.

"In the Age of
Globalisation,
positive differences
should be valued
rather than
homogenised.
It is this quality
which helped
establish Australian
writers such as
David Malouf,
Thomas Kenneally
and Robert Hughes.
Many Australian artists
have recognised
how differences
of perception of place
count for just so much
in understanding
who and what we are."

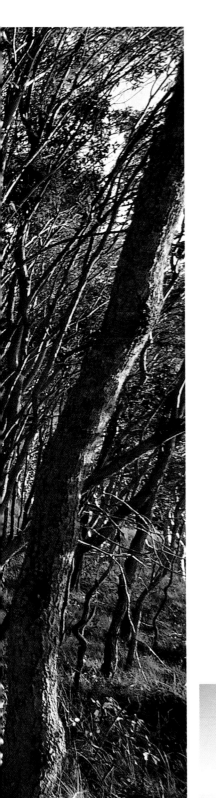

Opposite and below

Lightly wooded native coastal bush provides cues for lightweight construction techniques.

The gene pool was established in 1969 by Gabriel Poole at Buderim, 100 kilometres north of Brisbane. A one-time jackaroo and bush carpenter, Poole's practice blossomed along with the region as a tourist destination. In 1972 he employed, so fortuitously, Lindsay Clare. Three years later Kerry Clare arrived, followed in 1978 by John Mainwaring. A quarter of a century later, and working independently, this group, inadvertently, has become one of Australia's pre-eminent design centres. They have had to survive primarily on residential and small-scale commercial and public work, yet even provincial limitations have failed to thwart their ability to make a mighty impression. All are winners of major design awards, including the nation's highest accolade for residential design, and share more than fifty state and national awards. In 1998 Gabriel Poole was awarded the highest honour of the Gold Medal by the Royal Australian Institute of Architects. That the work of these three firms is of a similarly high standard is hardly coincidental. Having worked and played together, they share many ideals and sensibilities. Their designs are evocative, being characterised by the use of lightly draped materials. Their response to place is different; sometimes provocatively so and consistently out of step with residential, commercial and institutional development because it 'talks' less of mass and veneer and more about releasing the elements of breeze, light and shade. In doing so, there is a strong debt to simple, lightweight materials once spurned as inferior but now intrinsically part of an emerging design vocabulary.

There is a ring of such ambrosial decadence about a 'Sunshine Coast Group' that it will surprise many with its simple beauty. What sounds perilously like an excuse for lifestyle first and work a remote second, has become a workbench for an Australian idiom of particular originality. Many architectural practices have made an artform out of style without ever fully understanding the principles by which those results are achieved.

Until a decade ago, few people would have been brave enough to punt on any major creative force emanating from this region. By the late 1980s it was apparent there was a very definite rustling in the bushes and that something else was taking root far deeper than pineapples, bananas and sugarcane; something much more sublime and at least as productive. The lawless jumble of discount warehouses and random bulldozing of rainforest destined to make way for shelves of air-freshener, toilet rolls and canned fruit included other unexpected twists — architecture that converted the descriptive garnish of so many practices into a rare reality.

By world standards it has all the hallmarks of difference and as such it has attracted a level of international interest far beyond the resounding clatter and hyperbole generated by so many corporate architectural practices. The difference, of course, being predominantly small-scale work painstakingly crafted, sensitively sited and, very precisely, of the region. In the Age of Globalisation, positive differences should be valued rather than homogenised. It is this quality which helped establish Australian writers such as David Malouf, Thomas Kenneally and Robert Hughes. Many Australian artists have recognised how differences of perception of place count for just so much in understanding who and what we are.

The Sunshine Coast (population 240,000) still has remnants of paradise. It suffers from the usual excesses of poor planning associated with rapid population growth, but it retains areas of rare spectacle that encompass the vertiginous Glass House Mountains, originally noted in Captain Cook's diaries as Grass House Mountains but altered unknown to Cook. This dramatic group of volcanic plugs belched from the earth's crust some twenty-five million years ago is surrounded by a hinterland of gently rolling hills to create a lush green horizon joined to an enamelled horizon. Here and there, ancient cones breach the cane-fields and pineapple plantations. Just as there is an inevitability about the process of change, there is also a justifiable anxiety that in ten or twenty years time the landscape will be altered, irrevocably. At harvest time this sublime backdrop of pineapple plantations and sugarcane fields becomes a place

t retains an
nnocence only
made possible by
astute observation;
a feathered edge
no less remarkable
than a bird's wing,
a slender strut
seemingly borrowed
from the wing
of a dragonfly.
This is the language
of parts evolved that,
n so much of their
work, creates ease,
animation and
tension."

of machetes, machines and burnoffs as the sky turns acrid and the air sickly sweet. It heals quickly and will continue to do so until more suburbs and shopping strips are installed. To the east, the Pacific roars and fizzes as it un-scrolls.

There was a time, not so long ago, when Australians with little disposable income made an intuitive response with a fibro shack, slatted windows and corrugated iron roof. The canecutter's shack, stripped to bare necessity, exemplified this improvised utility best of all. The traditional 'Queenslander', one of Australia's few contributions to world architecture, is all but ignored as a passive energy design reference along the continent's Pacific Rim. 'Prestige' and 'commanding' are the buzz words of local real estate entrepreneurs. Architects, planners and developers are flat-out satisfying demand. Scalloped concrete pillars and ponderous, granosite-clad forms are the crudest echoes of glory. Many crave the prestige conferred by fantasies applied with Caesar in mind.

Two hundred and fifty kilometres south are tower blocks, fortress villas, fast food stalls, theme parks and stretched limos. In the absence of anything else, suburb names are unashamedly plucked, as a connoisseur contemplating a tray of truffles, from North America, to satisfy a perceived cultural hunger. Miami on the Gold Coast and Virginia near the Sunshine Coast are part of the expanding cultural waistline. This confused identity extends further. It applies to modern cities and suburbs everywhere and reaches an astonishing level of uncertainty and vulgarity along the entire east coast from Melbourne to Cairns. Gadget-packed homes virtually bereft of an environmental conscience hum, flush and whirr as though natural resources were only ever destined for rapid consumption.

Coupled with television, these communities are isolated in a benign, yet profound way, whereby a flickering box beams in a world of information, a ping pong ball of knowledge and a pin-head of wisdom. The global blender has taken away as much as it has given. It has homogenised and flattened

cultural differences. It has given us McDonald's in the most unexpected places and brought 'Melrose Place' and Oprah Winfrey into the lives of once remote tribespeople. Suddenly, we are all Neighbours. The electronic spell of mass communications also affects expectations in suburbia. Communities once mesmerised by glass beads are now captivated by the glass tube. Television references are now benchmarks. Contemporary western 'lifestyle' remains the ultimate ambition for people who no longer enjoy clear streams and a traditional diet. As cultures become dependent upon external economic forces, their authenticity and vitality evaporates. This is also the way of architecture. Production line design driven by economic rationalism provides a Trojan horse of hope for communities and societies that attempt to keep in touch with the rest of the world. Innocence and wonder are hijacked and brutally delivered into the twentieth century. In a vain attempt to bridge differences and link economies, habitats are handed over like cast-off clothes without regard for local conditions and cultural mores. This betrays an intuitive response to climate and a trust in that part of our brain that is encoded with the memory of older, but perhaps wiser, civilisations.

Despite the Coast's quick embrace of new styles and sensations, echoes of former lives crackle like scrub underfoot. Many of its Aboriginal placenames — Didillibah, Bli Bli, Mooloolaba and Beerburrum — chime to become single-word poems. These convey a joy and affection for places that supported hundreds of generations of indigenous people. In many instances, names are all that remain of the Dreamtime. It is fanciful to construct an idea whereby a group of architects from the late twentieth century in some way relate to Aboriginal mythologies, yet the gap narrows. We only need consider the regard for place as a starting point. As architects, they share a profound reluctance to make the land submissive to the built form. This starting point is contrary and fundamental to modern planning and building codes. The group also demonstrates resourcefulness by turning adversity to advantage. Gabriel Poole's tree-houses are

"It is fanciful to construct an idea whereby a group of architects from the late twentieth century in some way relate to Aboriginal mythologies, yet the gap narrows. We only need consider the regard for place as a starting point. As architects, they share a profound reluctance to make the land submissive to the built form."

Opposite and below
Lightweight forms in
substance and shadow
reveal the connection
between the natural
and built environment.

underpinned by remarkably unobtrusive structural systems. John Mainwaring's buildings are defined as much by their edges as their openings. The Clares provide an elegant, simple plan and materiality steeped in the craft tradition. A talent to identify and source local grassroots skills and materials is a further marker of work that connects all three practices to the spirit of indigenous cultures.

Contrary to so much design work that feeds off the vagaries of fashion, the Sunshine Coast Group has matured gradually to develop its own voice and identity. Their design language shares many core values of process, but the commonality of purpose and expression is altogether uncommon by Australian and world standards. So much so, that during the past decade, the North American and European design press have been stirred by examples of the group's work. Expanding international recognition should not come as a complete surprise. Architecture of such ephemeral lightness is a rarity in Europe and North America where the thundering scale of mansion stereotype, cluttered boutique apartments and ugly fads have left so many disillusioned with the profession. In many countries, restrictive building codes have plunged villages into a virtual time warp of country cottages and brass doorknobs.

The architect and critic Robin Boyd has come to symbolise a quality of agitation for change which has been beyond his contemporaries. Few other Australians are as passionate about their belief in place as the Sunshine Coast Group. Boyd was such a great champion of change and his work on Victoria's Mornington Peninsula in the early 1950s was a precursor to the Sunshine Coast in so many ways: 'This was holiday land; it was holiday time for architecture. The over-anxious architects had been left behind in the city. Here the plans were simple and free. Buildings were allowed to discard their stiff clothes; they went naked and unashamed and seemed to enjoy the sunshine.' There is a larrikin disregard in the group's attitude which largely rejects the fad of political correctness which can so easily

extinguish passionate opinion and creative force. An architecture of good manners too often results in a reluctance and inability to produce superior results.

Regarded by many in the profession as mavericks, their ostensibly envied lifestyle is one of tremendous rigour, self-discipline and long working hours. Despite their acclaim and recognition, commercial success has proved relatively modest — a result of an uncritical market lured by nostalgia and apparitions of paradise. So much development results from a fleeting visit in the style of a visiting celebrity whose impact is noisy but shallow. In contrast, Poole, Mainwaring and Clare Design have lived and breathed the Coast most of their lives. It must anger or disappoint more than they would care to admit when they observe the efforts of many interstate and overseas architects who are unwilling to or incapable of coming to terms with the place. The architects' own houses — Poole and Mainwaring live close to Noosa Heads, the Clares just south at Buderim — demonstrate the difference. Poole's triumvirate of pavilions appears to float like a hovercraft, Mainwaring deconstructs and invents an amphibious vernacular, while the Clares' envelope rejoices in the climate with material finesse.

The group's work carries on this evocation of opposites; of fragile, strong shelter. Comprised of finely draped layers instead of a single solid wall, the results feather and fragment materials to become an architecture of edges and openings. It is easily misunderstood as aberrant folly; of viewing transparency as somehow insubstantial and an inferior investment strategy alongside a solid brick box. Their preferred palette of materials — sheet steels, compressed cement sheet and plywood — cause gastric upset and palpitations among many lending institutions. No matter how dumb and unresponsive to climate and place, bricks have an irresistible appeal to bankers. They never heard Boyd's lament and still they fail to hear.

Long ago, Poole, Mainwaring and the Clares acquired a fascination with the ingenuity, craft and visual rhythms of architects of the calibre of Alvar

"Their design language shares many core values of process, but the commonality of purpose and expression is altogether uncommon by Australian and world standards. So much so, that during the past decade, the North American and European design press have been stirred by examples of the group's work. Expanding international recognition should not come as a complete surprise. Architecture of such ephemeral lightness is a rarity in Europe and North America where the thundering scale of mansion stereotype, cluttered boutique apartments and ugly fads have left so many disillusioned with the profession."

Below Coastal eucalyptus
and sclerophyll provide a
reference of strength and
delicacy.

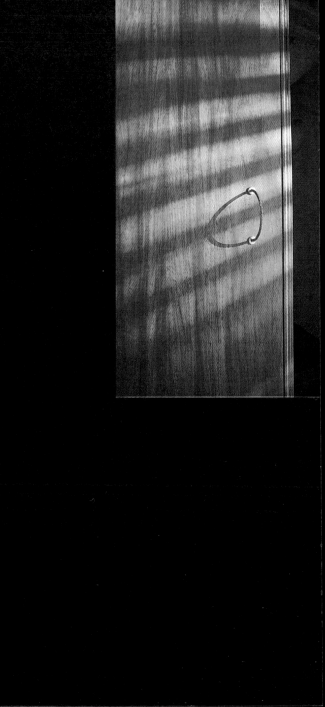

'Typically they revere the slender to the plump. Articulated edges and appropriately expressed envelopes are transferred to their interiors that use light to juxtapose shadow, animate space and reconcile climate. This atelier approach to construction effectively pre-dates the whip and mini-skirt of modernism. This minimalism resurrected the intensity, scale and rigour articulated by North American Shaker furniture at its apogee a century earlier."

Aalto, Mies van der Rohe and Renzo Piano. There is clearly an adaptation in much of the group's work, conscious or otherwise, of a preoccupation with the association of materials and forms. Typically they revere the slender to the plump. Articulated edges and appropriately expressed envelopes are transferred to their interiors that use light to juxtapose shadow, animate space and reconcile climate. This atelier approach to construction effectively pre-dates the whip and mini-skirt of modernism. This minimalism resurrected the intensity, scale and rigour articulated by North American Shaker furniture at its apogee a century earlier. Consistent with this approach, the group's work frequently incorporates prototype fixtures and fittings locally made to the architects' specifications, thus extending the architectonic vision. It encourages an appreciation of the many parts that reflect the handcrafted and machined components rooted variously in movements such as Shaker, École des Beaux-Arts and modernism.

To understand the differences is to appreciate the way each practice approaches its work. All three are driven by the way buildings are formed; the relationship, for example, of an eyelet to a handrail and, in turn, to a staircase. The relationship between various trades also allows for a suitable match of requirement and solution. It works in a very primary sense of understanding patterns of living and working so that spaces take on a relevance not widely grasped and too often only vaguely comprehended. Rather than boxed-in and reliant on refrigerated airconditioning for comfort levels, theirs resurrects the spirit of the holiday shack with its beachcomber simplicity. Sights, sounds and scents are treated as simple discoveries rather than sanitised and treated as ersatz experience in the manner of nervous tourists confronted by exotic disease or hostile climate. This is architecture less preoccupied with 'luxury' appointments and finishes than the palpable qualities of air, light and space. Expressed as a series of thin edges, their work frequently appears to bristle like the pages of an opened book. Rather than a single barrier or resolute box, their designs are typically attenuated and animated

by awnings, louvres and screens. But these are never add-ons in the vein of so much speculative housing riddled with throw-away references to an imagined subtropical environment. Treatments such as broad metal eaves project like hat brims to provide protection from sun and rain, as much as they heighten the experience of weather patterns to amplify the first patter of raindrops before the deluge.

This bond with lightweight materials largely springs from disparate points of the globe. Charles and Ray Eames's Case Study House at Pacific Palisades in Los Angeles (1948) fused an industrial language of prefabrication with Japanese minimalism and a Scandinavian finesse with sculptural timber furniture and interior finishes. The Eameses brought to bear a tremendous focus on detailing. This was most conspicuous in the machined bolt-together assembly as well as functional utility of their steel and plywood furniture. The Eames's ideal of modular flexibility based on the Japanese Edo, of a contemplative union with nature, has influenced successive generations of architects. Few, though, have interpreted the principles as effectively as the Sunshine Coast Group. Rather than merely appropriate the imagery, they have created a holistic architecture of pared, modular construction with a feeling of humanism.

Poole's Eumundi Tent House (1990), in the Noosa hinterland, perhaps best embodies the utilitarian envelope of ephemeral lightness and flexibility. Here is an architecture of infinite choice. Using a prototype, bolt-together, steel frame system, Poole pushes the building envelope to the point where walls virtually dematerialise in an effort to make a supreme connection with the environment. Poole's fascination with reading the climate allows an extraordinary degree of flexibility by simply opening or closing walls using retractable blinds. A vinyl or 'fly' roof and ceiling separated by a thermal zone of air helps produce an envelope that is cool in summer and warm in winter. The rice paper and bamboo Shoji screen is undoubtedly an influential precursor for the Eames as much as it is for these

"It works in a very primary sense of understanding patterns of living and working so that spaces take on a relevance not widely grasped and too often only vaguely comprehended. Rather than boxed-in and reliant on refrigerated airconditioning for comfort levels, theirs resurrects the spirit of the holiday shack with its beachcomber simplicity. Sights, sounds and scents are treated as simple discoveries rather than sanitised and treated as ersatz experience in the manner of nervous tourists confronted by exotic disease or hostile climate. This is architecture less preoccupied with 'luxury' appointments and finishes than the palpable qualities of air, light and space."

Right Light and shade
of the coast is referential
in the emblematic simplicity
of battened screens
and tent-like forms.

architects. Modified and adapted to define spaces and model views, such techniques and traditions have been absorbed and reinterpreted to produce a new vitality.

The stilt construction and verandah-style 'Queenslander' has helped to define a suitable climatic response of distinct, regional identity. Devices such as awnings, slats and *brise soleil* are consistently explored with a fine balance of lyricism and technique. Most of their residential and commercial projects are narrow-waisted to facilitate ventilation and natural light. Much of this work conveys the impression of travelling by luxury yacht with almost infinite variation for fine-tuning responsiveness to conditions. Careful detailing and handling of interiors conveys this same ambience and optimum space utilisation. These are not stylistic devices or contrivances, but are consistent with the approach that buildings of the region perform best without the usual ballast of concrete and roof tiles. Ceiling treatments, for instance, are given as much emphasis as floors and walls. Flared roofs, a trademark of Poole and Mainwaring especially, introduce light in a way that contributes towards a spatial quality manipulated by strategically placed windows and apertures.

Designing for such an environment should be relatively simple, yet clearly it is not. Expedience remains the predominant feature of market forces; thus, development cuts so many corners that the only real scope for individuality is the glam and tinsel that titillates interiors magazines. Why should anyone be straitjacketed by the ill-fitting design of an architect who has so easily surrendered to style? The group has actively participated in the political process to challenge the impoverished stereotype of coastal development. All three practices have rejected important prospects on this basis of principle. Having snared their architect of choice, some clients will demand a course utterly contrary to the architect's design spirit and sensibility. There is an obvious cachet in having any one of the three practices on board; a factor many developers recognise.

In an age when greed is back on the agenda and maximalism and status are so entwined, minimalism can be interpreted as a foolhardy or brave strategy. A preference for low-tech, lightweight and affordable materials is at odds with the majority of new housing development. Expensive, energy-sapping add-ons are rejected outright. They eschew fake, energy-conscious housing decorated with solar panels, satellite dishes and airconditioners. In the place of these they use natural ventilation devices, intelligent design and, of course, the power of light and shade.

'Architecture is a socio-political medium,' argues John Mainwaring. 'Just because this is the era of speculative project housing, I can't see why architects have to bend over backwards to be in context with that. If it's good architecture then it will polarise people. It will threaten their identity and possibly question their view of existence. We produce finishes that really contrast the fake, wedding cake exteriors pasted on like sugar and water.'

Mainwaring describes many Sunshine Coast houses as 'the monsters next door' and spears through the heart neighbouring estates he calls 'Death Valley'. Poole takes it a step further. He says there are 'a whole lot of buildings from around the place that I would love to blow-up . . . but first I have to buy them.' A fundamental difference between this and the group's approach is one of construction; of fretting less about the colour of granite benchtops and caring more about the assembly of structure; of putting substance before surface. Many home-buyers who choose the quick-fix, tilt slab construction are unfamiliar with the range of possibilities. Leaving behind their suburban fortress, few are prepared for the adventure of a life less cosseted from the 'terrors' of the natural world. For some, life is under twenty-four-hour push button control to complete the process of detachment and alienation until the next power failure.

Against the tide of client expectation and consumer demand, the group has pressed forward. In the process they have liberated many clients who would

Below Views north across Granite Bay framed by pandanus palm.

Opposite Chapman Residence, Noosaville, John Mainwaring.

Having snared their
architect of choice,
some clients will
demand a course
utterly contrary
to the architect's
design spirit
and sensibility.
There is an obvious
cachet in having
any one of the three
practices on board;
a factor many
developers recognise.
In an age when greed
is back on the agenda
and maximalism and
status are so entwined,
minimalism
can be interpreted
as a foolhardy
or brave strategy."

have otherwise been doomed to another life altogether. The Los Angeles architect Ed Niles, formerly a right hand of Case Study impresario Craig Ellwood, says of his role: 'My job is to help clients discover the other half of who they are.' And he does. Many of these clients are highly skilled in such areas as neuro-surgery and criminal law, but confess to an architecture-led awakening of their psyche. Few architects have this touch, but Poole, Mainwaring and the Clares have it. They all attract clients who are prepared to make this journey of self-discovery and who discover that architecture can be a doorway for discovery of the arts.

There is a palpable sense of *deja vu* and memory embedded in so much of this architecture. In large measure this is explained by the pervasive influence on each practice of Scandinavian architecture — in particular, that of Alvar Aalto. A powerful muse to so many architects, but, for this group especially, one that recalls the master alone confronting his own muse in a sub-Arctic world of summer brilliance and enforced winter gloom. Who else but Aalto could reconcile these climatic extremes with such delicate invention?

At no time does the architecture attempt to dominate or assert authority over its environment. Instead, he displays a fluency and optimism in its treatment of the natural world as central to human understanding of each other and its place. This was a land he revered rather than one to be forced into submission. Aalto was such a master of form and space that it speaks effortlessly and directly to those who experience it first hand. Rarely in architecture do we discover such spirituality and profound sense of place. Aalto's influence on the group's work comfortably transcends the more common appropriation of the master's chairs, light-fittings and vases to create a superficial Scandinavian ambience. Craft and restraint, two markers of Finnish design, are attitudes adopted by the Clares in particular. Restraint is certainly exemplified in the external expression of work by each practice. The ideas are so often refreshingly simple and their execution inevitably of moderation and understatement.

Finland and Queensland are utterly remote from each other in so many ways, yet a remarkable cultural transfer has occurred which has nothing to do with sycophancy and everything to do with adaptation to place. Australian suburbia is a place of ambiguity, shifting ground and redevelopment without any of the continuity understood by earlier generations. Finnish architecture is part of the national psyche in a way that would perplex most western communities. Architects such as Aalto are so revered that they end up headlining on national currency. This ability to deal without sentiment, with extremes of climate and light, social interaction and solitude, produces an architecture that inevitably becomes part of enriching people's lives. This philosophy provides the basis for an approach that treats architecture less as the deluxe option and more as one of necessity for physical comfort and emotional equilibrium.

Other influences prevail. This 'fraying' of edges and scrimming of views is not in itself highly original — many buildings in the tropics use shutters and awnings, and Japanese architecture is of course seminal in the process of achieving privacy and prospect. The thinness of the house is itself *engawa*, or Japanese 'verandah'. In such a culture the experience extends further — the luminous eyes of the geisha behind a rice paper fan, for instance. Japanese lore has it that the samurai blade was polished to such an edge that a leaf floating downstream could be halved merely by making contact with the steel. This reverence for the edge was not just practical — an opponent could be cleaved with half the effort of a blunt blade — but it added to the warrior's mystique and no doubt provided tactile and aesthetic pleasure for its owner. Translated to other times and climates, this definition and layering of materials is almost invariably interesting.

A principal influence for John Mainwaring is the work of Vienna-born Rudolph Schindler who, along with Richard Neutra, became precursors to Los Angeles Case Study Housing of the 1950s and 1960s. Working briefly for Frank Lloyd Wright, Schindler displayed an impressive gift for the articulation

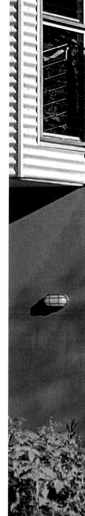

Poole has been relentless in his technical explorations, most notably with his Quadropod building system which provides an unobtrusive, modular steel chassis to effortlessly and economically straddle difficult building sites with minimal disturbance. The Gloster residence (1984) exemplifies the idea of structure sketched into nature. Building light is not merely a catchphrase."

of structure. His residential commissions projected a radiant clarity of vertical and horizontal space. The mass of masonry was effortlessly enlivened by walls of glass and flat, thin roofing. Even by today's standards, Schindler's Fitzpatrick house (1936) and Harris house (1942) crystallise a quite stunning modernity. The slender prefabrication of Charles and Ray Eames, as well as the mechanical platforms that projected so many Case Study houses to dizzy limits, provide Mainwaring and Poole with vital technical and creative cues. Progressively leaning even closer to delicacy and away from monument, Mainwaring polished his work with the precision and nuance of the Japanese vernacular to sublimate the raw experience of mere open plan space. These references from the Pacific Rim continue to inform much of the group's work.

It is difficult to overlook the Cubist influence of the de Stijl group on Poole. This sudden eruption of primary colour in a time of black and white film and pastel Impressionism was a shocking *tour de force*. Gerald Rietveld's stand-out chair of primary colours remains astonishing even today. Van Doesberg's attempts to translate art into architecture and Mondrian's graphic constructions of chromatic squares and grids vigorously explore life beyond the cube. De Stijl provided many artists and architects with a guidebook to travel outside of accepted boundaries. Poole has remained well outside the box ever since he discovered his own 'voice' after turbulent times in the late 1970s. Some candid self-appraisal helped overcome a period when, driven by developers, his architecture appeared to have peaked well short of its promise. During the 1960s, Poole worked for, and came under the influence of, the Queensland modernists Robin Gibson and John Dalton. Gibson's floating white Cubist constructions exemplified by meticulous detailing were complemented by Dalton's residentially derived architecture that investigated natural ventilation and light. Dalton's Mediterranean influence incorporated courtyards, sloping roofs, screens and slatted window treatments.

Absorbing selected elements from each designer, and recognising limitations as well as strengths, Poole identified the best elements and merged these into his own. This has resulted in a great regard for composition and harmony coupled with an evocation of landscape. Poole has been relentless in his technical explorations, most notably with his Quadropod building system which provides an unobtrusive, modular steel chassis to effortlessly and economically straddle difficult building sites with minimal disturbance. The Gloster residence (1984) exemplifies the idea of structure sketched into nature. Building light is not merely a catchphrase.

More recently, Los Angeles architecture has had an influence. The playfulness and growing confidence of Frank Gehry, Morphosis, Eric Moss and Frank Israel, along with Hank Koning and Julie Eizenberg, provide parallels with the Sunshine Coast Group. Driven to challenge the excess of banality and social dislocation all around, these urban architects have demonstrated a creative response to their environment. Hinged on a fault line, architectural elegance can be capriciously reduced to rubble. This LA work echoes a toughness and grit of rioting and social dislocation. Is it any wonder that this should be the birthplace of startling urban forms wrenched and twisted into an engaging impermanence of deconstruction? It is difficult here to know which is worse, the mutant spread of the city without intelligent density, or the coiling rip-cord of freeways which appear as a spiralling noose in the absence of real public transport options. For the aficionado at least, some redemption is offered by the LA Group and its modernist forerunners including Pierre Koenig and John Lautner. In an Australian context, the Sunshine Coast Group has worked in a parallel time frame and, given time, may be seen as no less important to this region of the world.

Poole's Lake Weyba residence (1996) is a high point of authenticity, being so easily connected to the land and yet one step removed from the usual organic variety. This triumvirate of pavilions is installed

Below The Glasshouse Mountains provide a totemic anchor to the rolling hinterland.

Opposite Much of the Australian 'Bush' is coastal and, unlike most Asian and European flora, allows the eye to penetrate and read through foliage — a condition frequently utilised by the Sunshine Coast Group.

Below
Porcellini Residence,
Flaxton, Noosa Hinterland,
Clare Design.

Right
The French Quarter,
Noosa Heads,
John Mainwaring.

Opposite
Canal House,
Noosa Waters,
John Mainwaring.

The group's palette of materials is usually light steel or timber framing, steel or cement sheet cladding, with plywood and natural timbers used internally. Trying to tease apart and distinguish difference between the work of the three practices is not simple. Similarities are inevitable given the unavoidable cross-pollination, shared environment and philosophical platform."

in the manner of sculpture. It has an evocative materiality with its references to tents, pavilions, bath houses and verandahs in a single structure. Its layers of polycarbonate, steel and ply sheathe its frames in a similar way to skin stretched over bone. Roller shutter blinds on the northern vertical face of the living/kitchen pavilion coupled with retractable walls produce a luxury of options in climate control. In elevation the rhythms of light and line are conspicuous in their delicacy.

The argument that architect-designed buildings perpetuate elitism is only true when they become extravagant on price. High-quality design need not plunge anyone into a black hole of debt. Poole's 'Capricorn 151' series of houses reveals how affordable, flexible and appropriate housing has become. Few architects have taken up the challenge of affordable, quality housing at a moderate entry-level price. The 'Capricorn' is the result of an unfolding lineage of 'exploratory' housing which includes his early Quadropod houses, the Tent House (1990) and the Lake Weyba residence (1996). The result is sublime simplicity. An elevated pavilion comprises a lightweight portal frame system, bolted timber bearers and plywood beams. Broad eaves, turbine ventilators and adjustable wall ventilation blades provide a low-maintenance, high-efficiency solution for climate and place. Three bedrooms, bathroom and laundry are at one end, with kitchen, dining and living areas at the other. At the heart, and connecting the two parts, is a skylit breezeway that epitomises Poole's bush spirit of minimal enclosure. Although not specifically intended for Aboriginal communities, the 'Capricorn' series provides a genuinely responsive alternative to the nightmarish boxes imposed by a succession of government bureaucrats.

The group's palette of materials is usually light steel or timber framing, steel or cement sheet cladding, with plywood and natural timbers used internally. Trying to tease apart and distinguish difference

between the work of the three practices is not simple. Similarities are inevitable given the unavoidable cross-pollination, shared environment and philosophical platform.

This lightness of touch is characterised by excellent passive energy performance and the perspective of a tree-house in preference to the cave. These are buildings to catch breezes, light and outlook. It is of little surprise when clients refer to the joy and delight that comes from the experience of such residential and commercial work. Spatial experience is derived from the tectonic and tactile. Living, dining and kitchen spaces are frequently merged and delineated not by walled compartments, but by a language of screens, beams, fin walls and floor insets, for example. Vertical connection between floor levels is frequently employed to create voids for air movement, balanced natural light and improved community. Such an ordering and hierarchy of spaces is driven by the relationship and needs of each residential or commercial client. This translates as thinner building envelopes, often expressed as insulated sheet steels, compressed fibre cement sheet and plywood, with careful fenestration to provide the calculated glimpse as much as the panorama. In this way, the social and cultural function of a building can take account of such issues as eye contact with children playing, guests arriving, meals preparation and privacy needs.

The similarities of approach and solution are reflected dramatically in the bristling roof of the University of the Sunshine Coast Library (1997, in conjunction with Lawrence Nield), designed and constructed 80 kilometres away in virtual isolation, yet simultaneously with Poole's Lake Weyba residence. Such coincidence of *leitmotiv* occurs because of the essentially gradual, evolutionary nature of each firm's work and the shared comprehension, if not varying interpretation, of specific design principles. It is only on closer inspection that the differences begin to reveal themselves. Mainwaring breaks up 'the rational box'

Opposite The University of the Sunshine Coast Recreation Building was produced by Clare Design in a sixteen-week turnaround from design to completion.

Right Stepped treatment of Rainbow Shores by the Clares allows optimum site utilisation and expansive sea views.

The Clares' work
illustrates elegance,
order and
rational space.
What is more,
it has that very
regional quality of
architects who really
understand their
place of work
instead of what
arrives via boardroom
hustling and slippery
salesmanship.
The design appears
as half glider and half
jump jet. Yet for all of
this, it is a pragmatic,
functional structure,
deftly layered to
provide lightweight
shelter of great poise
and elegance."

in unexpected and inventive ways. Poole oscillates between work that plugs into the earth or floats free.

Although of modest dimensions, all produce work that is crafted and visually coherent. The Clares' University of the Sunshine Coast Sports and Recreational Building (1997) is a frisbee-throw from the USC library icon and it demurs beautifully without being humbled in the process. The result is an instinctive and intuitive one that reflects just how well this partnership understands the relationship between buildings and people. The Clares' work illustrates elegance, order and rational space. What is more, it has that very regional quality of architects who really understand their place of work instead of what arrives via boardroom hustling and slippery salesmanship. The design appears as half glider and half jump jet. Yet for all of this, it is a pragmatic, functional structure, deftly layered to provide lightweight shelter of great poise and elegance. It is difficult to imagine more energy packed into a structure of such modest dimensions. Sleek, linear and vigorously animated, the result offers a seductive respite from the climatic friction of sun and storm.

Poole and Mainwaring are a restless part of the design and building process. Mainwaring is typically overt and carries an idea until it becomes a lyrical, emotive response. He is a master of the invented vernacular. His half wall, half roof, for example, becomes a 'woof' which he suggests will provide a visual defence 'against the elephant that goes in next door'. Poole relies heavily on an intuitive touch to the extent that his hits are spectacular while the few misses hang on grimly. Lindsay and Kerry Clare take a more rational approach to design to achieve a less volatile, more predictable outcome. Their work exalts the idea of a carefully conceived plan as the armature around which subsequent work turns.

Poole's work appears highly rational, yet it has enough irrational elements to keep everyone hanging on the edge for the result. Poole's work is also intuitive, but the physical manifestation is quite rational. The Clares argue convincingly that their solutions work with an apparent minimum of effort. Nevertheless, they achieve an extraordinary degree of resolution by modifying systems that are largely in place. Their strategy is less one of going to extreme lengths for mercurial effect, than of ensuring force through simplicity.

The Clares' work is frequently perceived as more restrained than either Poole's or Mainwaring's. 'That's good and bad,' says Lindsay Clare. 'It can be a compliment, but it can also mean we aren't trying hard enough to stretch ourselves.' Kerry Clare says of her one-time boss: 'Gabriel fluctuates enormously. He does heavy buildings and light ones. He's highly capable across the board and seems to love the challenge that different personalities and budgets provide. Finding the direction is very much part of it. Gabriel is now playing around with more masculine projects which we always knew he could do. He will have a go at it even when all the forces are working against him. He is still able to get fun out of them.' Mainwaring is regarded by Kerry Clare as finding a new edge: 'John's work is now much more controlled. His buildings have always been very spirited but you often looked at that early work and realised something was weighing it down or falling over. He's just made this subtle shift and the spirit is still there but you see much more competence in his handling of materials. And they're most definitely his buildings. We always tried to be, and have probably been, more precious about who we take on and that's limited our output. John puts himself right out there and pushes materials in a way which is very brave and he has created a strong niche.'

Lindsay Clare says a hypothetical design competition between the three firms would result in the following: 'Gabriel would almost certainly deliver the adventurous structural solution. John would try to do something from left field, quite hybrid and unpredictable, while we would work very hard to make it all appear very simple and easy. Importantly, you would enjoy being in each one of those buildings. That's what ties us all together; the aspiration and creation of a place for the occupants' pleasure. That would be the common link.'

"Mainwaring is typically overt and carries an idea until it becomes a lyrical, emotive response. He is a master of the invented vernacular."

Left and above
Soaring steel columns, angles, purlins and struts provide a forest of fabrication at the University of the Sunshine Coast Library, by John Mainwaring and Lawrence Nield.

John's work
is now much
more controlled.
His buildings have
always been
very spirited
but you often
looked at that early
work and realised
something was
weighing it down
or falling over.
He's just made
this subtle shift
and the spirit is
still there but you
see much more
competence in his
handling of materials.
And they're most
definitely his
buildings."

Previous Palms soar
in the south-west alcove
of the University of the
Sunshine Coast Library.

Right Skiffs provide a cue
for the thinness of edge
and strength to be found in
John Mainwaring's Canal
Residence, Noosa Waters.

"Instead of pursuing
major public projects,
individual interests have,
of necessity,
centred on residential
and small-scale
public buildings.
There is a simple
philosophy behind
all of this. It has
helped retain creative
control in the way
that parents committed
to their children do
in the hope that
they will become
good adults.
Many major public
buildings are so
ill-considered that
they quickly become
delinquent and derelict.
Not enough mothering
on the drawing board,
inadequate fathering
in design development
and, finally,
insufficient love."

Within this relaxed, loose ambience one senses that the architecture is never arbitrary or slack. It illustrates that a disciplined approach is a fundamental asset in the production of a structure which provides great pleasure simply because of its flexibility and expressed balsawood, model aircraft, method of assembly. No single design by any architect has anything that approaches universal application. Architecture can provide a crucial difference when it demonstrates a wider relevance and affordability. Regrettably, some draughting services have hijacked elements of the group's work and done everyone a disservice. This simple downloading of the peripherals without ever understanding the importance of process can only undermine the genuine article. Their work should not be sabotaged by such short-sighted flattery. Hopefully, in more skilled hands, their work will more fully unfold and travel to a far wider audience. Invariably, as other architects and clients absorb these directions, the principles that architects such as Aalto, Schindler and others worked so hard for will be re-sown further afield.

Landmark architecture has the capacity to impress because of its scale and cost, but it so often bears little relationship to how we live and make our lives. This is why these three practices are so important. In fifty years time, much of the group's work will disappear under the jungle of urban growth. So much of this architecture has a fleeting, evanescent quality. Little of it seems to place great faith in rock-solid permanence as much as in the delight provided during its lifetime. This is the theme that permeates its work. Instead of pursuing major public projects, individual interests have, of necessity, centred on residential and small-scale public buildings. There is a simple philosophy behind all of this. It has helped retain creative control in the way that parents committed to their children do in the hope that they will become good adults. Many major public buildings are so ill-considered that they quickly become delinquent and derelict. Not enough mothering on the drawing board, inadequate fathering in design development and, finally, insufficient love.

In stark contrast, Poole, Mainwaring and the Clares create architecture of 'thoughtfulness, humility, love and perhaps, above all, conviction'. Instead of growing rich through compromise and cynicism, the trio has stuck by its principles. This should all prove ultimately embarrassing in juxtaposition to the status-conscious palazzo, but, alas, taste is so often exquisitely bulletproof. They are not the first architects to turn their backs on more lucrative prospects to cultivate architecture of integrity, but few demonstrate such defiance of profit before principle. After all, this is architecture made hugely relevant to so many Australians because it is affordable and within reach. So much for the perception that architecture is only for the bosom of an elite.

The course of talent is so often deflected, and sometimes made poignant, by irony. Because of a sluggish local economy and desire to take on projects of greater scale and substance, the Clares have put their office into cruise control and have temporarily moved south as design directors with the New South Wales Government Architects Office in Sydney. Both have also been appointed adjunct professors of architecture at the University of Sydney. They have already made a very real impact. Mainwaring is principal architect of the Brisbane Mall redevelopment and continues his small practice producing inventive, regional work but worrying, always, about the next commission. Poole retains a solid client, base and the recognition of an RAIA Gold Medal has only added lustre and 'bankability'. For all of their considerable achievements, none has reaped anything approaching commensurate financial rewards. Money is not regarded as 'dirty stuff' but, equally, it is not their obsession.

"In stark contrast,
Poole, Mainwaring
and the Clares
create architecture
of 'thoughtfulness,
humility, love
and perhaps,
above all, conviction'.
Instead of
growing rich
through compromise
and cynicism,
the trio has stuck
by its principles.
This should all
prove ultimately
embarrassing
in juxtaposition to
the status-conscious
palazzo, but, alas,
taste is so often
exquisitely bulletproof."

e should also remember that the group's influence
xtends far beyond the pages of architecture and
estyle magazines. During the past two decades,
umerous architects have worked directly with,
nd come under the influence of, the group and
any of these have been profoundly influenced.
oole, Mainwaring and the Clares have been highly
ocal on a broad range of issues in their efforts to
nprove our quality of life. They are often outspoken
nd suffer the consequences of ruffling feathers.
his is the price of challenging mediocrity and
hallmark of all passionate talent.

nderlying their agitation and fire in the belly is
ork vital to Australia's sense of self and national
entity. As the nation ponders how it might cope
ith the responsibilities of becoming a republic
— of growing out of adolescence into adulthood —
uch architecture can help Australians rediscover
emselves. Through so much of our art and
erature we have been taught to critically examine
nd reappraise. The architecture of the Sunshine
oast is crucial to this process of growing up;
f understanding who we are and becoming whole.
this most unlikely of places, these architects are
nrowing down a challenge to popular perceptions
f national identity. This product of inspired labour
ngs and rumbles like all great art. Here, then,
re authentic Australian voices. Multiplied many times,
he' has become a 'they' of 'brothers'-in-arms.
he simplest of songs has built to a chorus.
time, it may even become an anthem.

Peter Hyatt

Below
McWilliam Residence,
Alexandra Headland,
Clare Design (1990).

Architecture for the people

"For a long time I have put in enormous effort
for minimal return in an endeavour to access
and influence the domestic market. I have had
a real desire to reclaim the initiative for the
profession and exert an influence that should
be architecture's natural responsibility."

Gabriel Poole

What is an architect's philosophy? To me it is probably my life, the things that have happened, the people I have met and those who have moved through it, my expectations, my aspirations, my family, my loves and my loyalties. All have contributed to the way I view architecture and what I believe it should contribute to our society. Our architecture should house people in surroundings that will enrich their lives and respond to their personal wants and needs. Each house should be tailored to the individual or family concerned.

My further philosophy is that as architects we should endeavour to raise the general standard of housing throughout our country, for it is this area that I view as being most sorely neglected by the profession. It is this area which I perceive as being hijacked by developers of mass housing, and it is condemning people to live in what I consider to be generally inferior accommodation. The public may not consider it so, because as architects we have failed to penetrate the market with economic housing recognisable as such and accepted as real housing.

For a long time I have put in enormous effort for minimal return in an endeavour to access and influence the domestic market. I have had a real desire to reclaim the initiative for the profession and exert an influence that should be architecture's natural responsibility. The fact that this isn't a God-given right is not God's fault, it is the profession's.

Opposite Dappled shade and a finely layered envelope.

Below The Lake Weyba House — a technical and poetic exploration.

I am now marketing a range of houses under the banner of 'Capricorn 151', which are ostensibly lightweight project houses. We are presently signing up two per week and interest is coming from all over Australia. Although designed for the tropics and subtropics, the system can be modified to accommodate climatic conditions in most parts of Australia. My aim is to continually modify and upgrade the product in response to public feedback. The 'Capricorn' series is affordable, well-designed, and winning recognition as an acceptable, even desirable, form of housing.

The challenge now is to keep my practice going, create a niche in general housing and claim some part of the mass market in the name of architecture. Hopefully, I can convince other architects to take up the challenge and follow suit. In doing so we will provide architecture instead of merely building and, for many, greatly improve their quality of life. If I can achieve that, then I will consider that the profession in which I have chosen to expand my life has been well served and that my stay on this planet has not been completely in vain.

Finally, I would like my buildings to be sustainable and 'eco-friendly' with the hope that we can place people carefully within our landscapes to avoid the destruction and havoc which accompanies large-scale housing developments.

Opposite The Tent House, Eumundi (1990).
The sublime connection of structure and environment. Walls are fully retractable vinyl, cyclone rated.

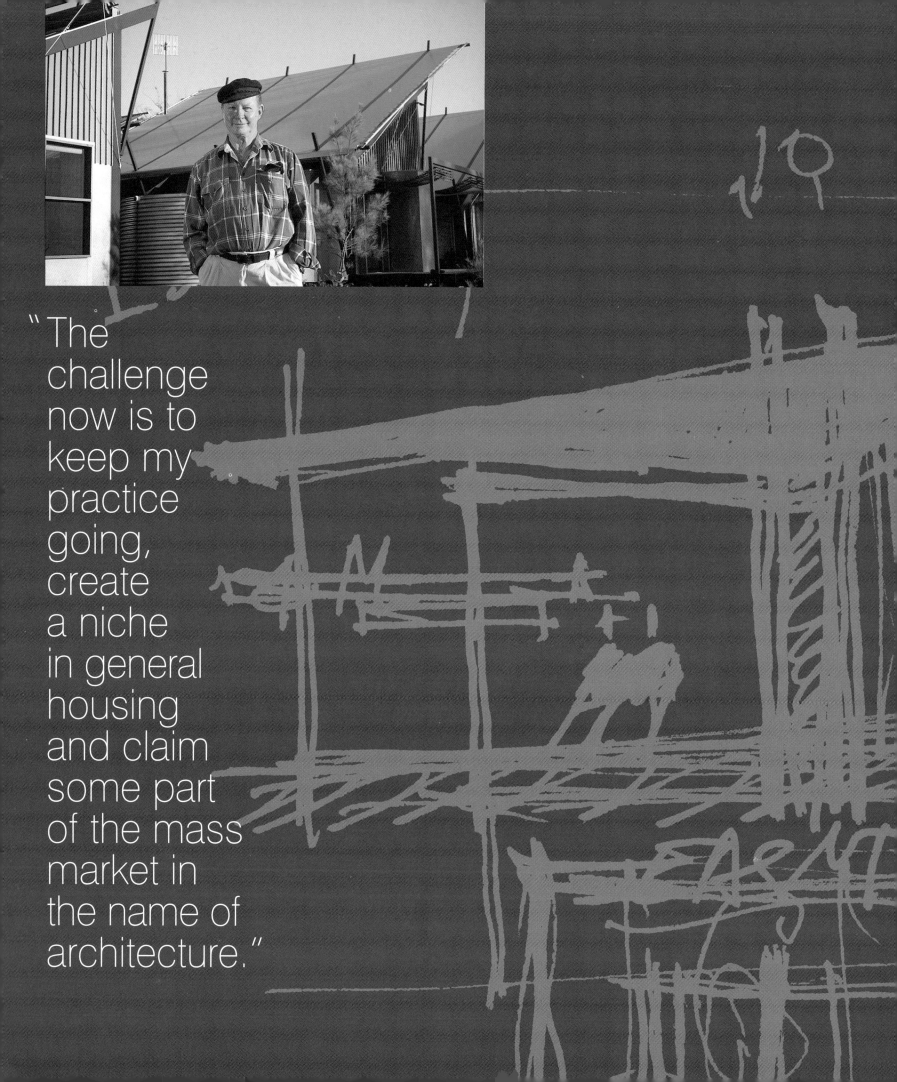

"The challenge now is to keep my practice going, create a niche in general housing and claim some part of the mass market in the name of architecture."

Gabriel Poole

Gloster Residence Noosa Heads 1984

Michael Gloster wandered down the narrow track on an equally narrow ridge between two gullies, to the first small Quadropod house at Lot 105, Noosa Valley Drive. Michael, a non-practising architect, was interested to inspect my new system with a view to using it for his own house, on land adjoining the national park at Noosa. He particularly liked the form of the under-floor system which, to his mind, related to the tree forms within the park.

He decided he would like to go ahead using the system, and asked if I would work with him to design the house. The principal innovation he was suggesting, was to build in the area under the house and within the confines of the pod towers, to be used as office space for him and his wife Glen, a landscape architect.

The building was to be supported on four towers of identical form and size and was a forerunner to the 'Capricorn 105' systems house. Walls would be constructed with light steel framing, panels timber framed with V-joint sheeting externally and fixed to the steel frame from the inside, virtually eliminating the need for scaffolding.

The same system was applied to the lower floor area, with walls taken to the head rails of the towers and the space from there to the underside of the floor. We then fitted clear fixed glass panels to retain transparency and the desirable forms of the adjustable Quadropod areas.

Double and single columns with adjustable arms were used, as with 'Capricorn 105', to construct external decks, and the addition of an external circular stair provided access between floors. Standard gang nail timber trusses framed the roof, which was corrugated sheet steel, to the ridge vented at both ends as a means of relieving internal pressure in the event of cyclones.

The house comprises a bedroom with ensuite and walk-in robe, living/dining room, kitchen and external decks to the upper floor. The lower floor accommodates Michael and Glen's offices, and the small room on the lower level is used for storage and guests.

Below Sketched into the bush the house projects into the tree tops.

Opposite left Casement pivot windows become air scoops to capture and direct air flow.

Opposite right End elevation reveals the tree house spirit and structural finesse of the Quadropod system.

Over page A seminal design from Poole at a time when most Australian architects remained anchored to the land. Passive ventilation systems provide a wide range of comfort options.

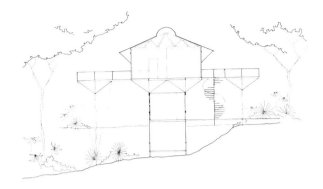

Opposite Poetic assembly. Minimal mass, maximum performance.

Below Poole maintains supreme transparency through sub-floor trusses and bracing.

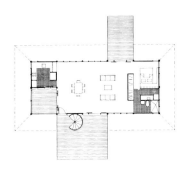

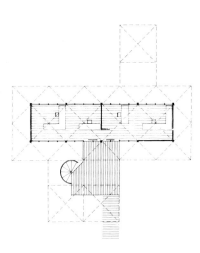

Noble Residence Noosa Hill 1985–86

Dave Noble was bobbing about in a small boat, fishing line in hand, just off Noosa Heads in Laguna Bay. Pointing to Noosa Hill, he said to his fishing mate: 'I own a block of land right up near the top of that hill and I can't get anyone to build a house on it for me.' His mate said, 'Well, there is a crazy architect called Gabriel Poole who has been building houses on difficult sites with a system he has designed and called "the Quadropod".' David and Pam Noble came to see me and the friendship endures to this day.

The house sits on essentially the same under-floor system as the Gloster house; however, this time we separated it into two free-standing towers. We increased the towers from a 3 metre module to a 3.6 metre module and similarly extended the floor framing to create 7.2 metre modules. We then placed these modules 3.6 metres apart. This provided free space between the modules which in future houses — Walker and Towers (1989) and Gartner (1990) — allowed us to install the necessary internal staircases for internal transition between floors.

Perched high on the hillside, this house was built without recourse to mechanical digging equipment or formal scaffolding. In this instance we created two floors over the platform and resorted to curved roofs. The RHS (rolled hollow sections) frame was retained and, with the exception of minimal walls for privacy, the building is basically glass.

The main building comprises entry decks and sundeck to the northern end, living/dining, kitchen, laundry, bathroom and two bedrooms on the lower floor, with the main bedroom, ensuite and dressing room on the upper floor. Located at the street frontage is a more conventional structure housing two carports and a garage. The custom orb roof of this building has been formed on an inverted curve to pick up the road gradient.

Below Supreme transparency through filigree structure. If proof was needed of Poole's arrival as an architect to follow, this was it. The modular tree-house.

Opposite A floating platform pared of structural baggage and braced for exceptional stability. A water-bird among the reeds.

Over page Having excelled with the Gloster Residence, Poole took an even more audacious step with the Noble House.

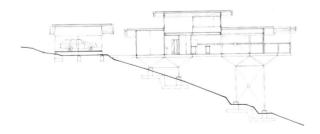

opposite top Details
reinforce the broader
concept and visual
rhythms.

opposite Forms remain
rather light and functional
with little evidence of
caprice or whimsy.

below Part hovercraft,
part yacht, subtle nautical
references help animate
surfaces.

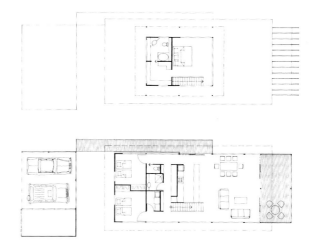

Gartner House Mt Tambourine 1990

On a visit to Noosa Heads, Angela Gartner saw a number of my houses and the partially completed Noble house. She came to my office and told me how much she admired my work. 'Gabriel, one day I'll have one of your houses. At the moment I haven't got the money, but when I have I'll come back to see you!' A couple of years later she walked back into my office and said, 'I now have the money and a piece of land at Mt Tambourine. Let's design a house.'

Angela is an artist. The land she selected was a spectacular rainforest site on a steep slope, dropping almost vertically some hundreds of feet to the valley below, and with views to the east overlooking the Gold Coast and the Pacific Ocean. Angela had now watched a number of Quadropod houses going up and she selected elements from each.

From the Gloster house she used the under-floor area within the Quadropod towers to place two bedrooms, a bathroom and laundry. We connected to the main floor by separating the towers, which provided space for the internal stair; but we took the system further and tacked an extra leg and one-quarter section of a tower to the back of each tower on a diagonal angle, forming triangular sections to the western side of what now became very distinct living modules to the house. One contained a large living/dining area and the other, Angela's studio in the triangle, plus her bedroom, dressing room, ensuite and spa.

The central division created to house the stair also accommodated the kitchen. A 3 metre wide deck ran north/south of this building on the eastern side, looking to the ocean. The main structure was once again steel framed and infilled to the east with glass, and on most other elevations with rough-sawn cedar weatherboards.

Angela had liked the custom orb Asian-style roofs used in my mother's house at Noosa and the Allen house at Dayboro, and requested that her roof be of this form, with the further request that we provide some form of clerestory lighting at the apex. The resulting structures feature parallel set steel beams with glazing between to create beautiful forms both inside and out and wonderful interiors of space and light.

Because Angela required a sense of security, we connected the house back to the top of the site with a suspended bridge and made the bridge only accessible through electronically opened doors to the garage. Angela, too, has become a close friend. With her impeccable taste, the house is always a delight to visit.

Opposite and below

The concave roof form of the Noble Residence is employed again but effectively mirrored to produce an Asian-style roof. Note steel bracing incorporated into window treatments to minimise structural vibration.

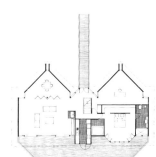

Right The now customary, Quadropod frame allows the precipitous site to be handled with relative ease. Lightweight construction materials allow for accurate prefabrication and minimal site disturbance.

Below and opposite Access is solely by means of a footbridge which provides the key circulation spine from the garage, culminating in a galley-style kitchen.

Tent House Eumundi 1990

We purchased twenty wonderfully wild hectares of what we found to be pretty much Aboriginal sacred ground, five minutes drive west of Eumundi, backed by a large hill, looking north across farmland and bordered on the west by the sacred Mt Bewah.

'Build me a simple weatherboard shack,' requested Elizabeth, my partner. After some colourful discussion she revised the request. 'OK, then, what's the simplest structure we can put here?' I innocently suggested a tent. 'OK, build me a tent.' We would have run a thousand kilometres the other way had we realised what we were letting ourselves in for.

Before we started building, I had a vicious and very painful bout of shingles to my head and face. We built a prototype of the tent (to be Lizzie's studio), and lived in it while we built the 'full-on' version. The 'spirits' sent down floods that washed out our roads and made the site inaccessible. In the middle of the night, they exploded our water tank.

Finally, with the assistance of the wonderful team we had working for us, we completed the project. It was truly a joy, and a wonderful and extraordinary living experience. Light steel frames moved like yacht spas in the wind, and the translucent roofs created ever-changing patterns of light and shade. With the floating tent forms, the inner roof of blue canvas, air gap and outer fly of white PVC, tensioned and lashed to light steel roof bows, cool space was created within the building.

Roll-up walls and windows and clear vinyl sliding doors opened our home to the environment and created a living experience like no other I had known. It caught the imagination of a nation and won our Institute's highest award for domestic architecture.

The *Sunday Mail* purchased a replica and erected it in the Brisbane Botanical Gardens and opened it to the public. It was raffled and some 60,000 people visited. We had more than 3000 enquiries and no jobs; it all but put us out of business. It was the Tent House.

Opposite and below

Australia's architecture entry in the 1991 Venice Biennale. The Tent House conveys a spirited, festive quality. Assembly took just one day.

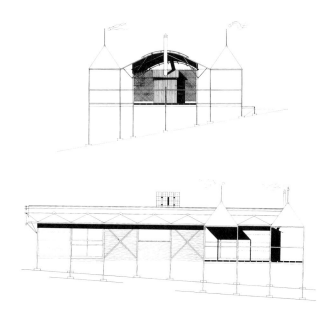

Opposite Rainforest and
former banana plantation
provide a backdrop.

Right and below
A double skinned vinyl roof
with retractable vinyl walls
stretched over a slender
steel frame.

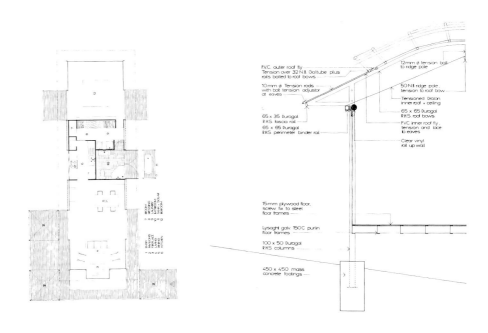

PVC outer roof fly
Tension over 32 N.B. Galtube plus
rails bolted to roof bows

12mm ø tension bolt
to ridge pole

10mm ø Tension rods
with bolt tension adjustor
at eaves

50 N.B ridge pole
tension to roof bow

65 x 35 Duragal
RHS fascia rail

Tensioned Dralon
inner roof + ceiling

65 x 65 Duragal
RHS perimeter binder rail

65 x 65 Duragal
RHS roof bows

PVC inner roof fly
tension and lace
to eaves

Clear vinyl
roll up wall

15mm plywood floor,
screw fix to steel
floor frames

Lysaght galv 150C purlin
floor frames

100 x 50 Duragal
RHS columns

450 x 450 mass
concrete footings

Poole House Lake Weyba 1996

The land situated at the western end of Lake Weyba, approximately ten minutes drive from Noosa Heads, is typically coastal wallum, with soft grass that grows to about 60 centimetres in height, and through which, over the course of the year, an ever-changing array of native flowers, gums, casuarinas and grass trees grows in profusion. Throughout the area the natural beauty is being overtaken by relentless development. It is feasible that in future our property may be the only surviving example of wallum for many kilometres.

We purchased the site while we lived in Sydney. The first design was really just an updated version of the Tent House, with more solid walls and roof structures and the inclusion of a custom orb lap pool.

When I decided I would like to have an office in the building, Lizzie requested that the bedroom be separated from the main house and suggested a variation from swimming pool to a large bath. Her further observation was that the land was not large enough for real privacy and that eventually the beautiful views we presently enjoyed over the wallum would be built out and lost. She suggested that the only view that could not be destroyed would be of the sky, and requested that I design a house that retained sky views from every room. This has been accomplished so that, even from the toilet, the sky can be observed and enjoyed.

From this revised brief we developed the new house in three modules connected by covered ways. The large front module contains living, dining/kitchen and my office, with a 3 metre wide deck running the full length of the building. The second module contains the bathroom with semi outdoor shower, with a clear acrylic roof to the sky, a large bath 3 metres long by 2 metres wide, specifically for the purpose of cooling off in our hot summer weather. Alcoves project from the walls to provide storage cupboards, while a large internal cupboard houses washing machine and dryer. A composting toilet, with heavenly outlook, is located on the opposite wall.

This second module is pretty much the engine room of the house and it is not uncommon to find two to three people in the room at any one time. It seems to suit our lifestyle. The last bedroom module is a bedroom only, with day beds located in alcoves on either side.

The house was designed around a series of structural frames of lightweight steel portals, spread at 2.4 metre intervals and lifted clear of the ground so that the pavilions 'float' above the native grass base. Walls are timber-framed and clad on the outside with precisely folded flat galvanised iron sheet, giving the building the appearance of being sculpted out of a solid metal block.

Windows are framed with heavy section treated timber with fixed insect screening, and sashes fabricated of aluminium flyscreen sections, glazed with clear vinyl and running vertically through the bottoms of the timber frames on the outside face of the walls. They are operated with a system of cords and light pulley blocks.

Large vertical sliding doors between the internal areas of the main pavilion and the verandah are similarly constructed and are operated by means of pulleys and counterweights in similar fashion to double-hung windows. The northern walls above 2.1 metres are simple inset screen timber frames, and these are weatherproofed by a standard garage roller-door mounted above the roof and operated by means of a hook on a long stick — very sophisticated!

Below A true pavilion house. Ephemerally light, open and climate responsive.

Opposite North facing, the front pavilion utilises six garage roller-doors to manage ventilation and light levels.

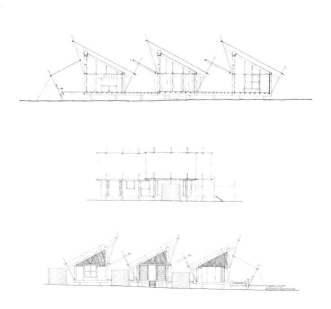

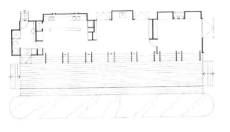

Opposite right Spa/pool and deck.

Opposite below A central deck provides a circulation spine that links the three modules.

Below Master bedroom reveals its lightweight construction. Note inner PVC roof. A 50mm gap between inner and outer layers allows rapid heat dissipation and thermal efficiencies in the style of a tent 'fly' cover.

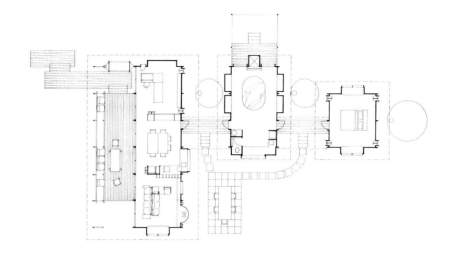

Pasternak Residence
Sunshine Beach 1996–97

These clients, new to Australia, required a substantial house of simple sophistication. They brought with them elegant furniture and chattels and, most importantly, two small children. We designed a beachside family home built on an exclusive group title estate that nestles into the sand dunes on the edge of a coral sea.

The site was small and the house, of necessity, covered it in its entirety. The house was further constrained by the 8 metre maximum height limit. This was once again very much venturing into the heavyweight building type. By following the hill slope with the air flow and taking the house through a series of voids, I was able to maintain the air circulation I required. Air finally filters behind the glass panel over the kitchen and follows the curved rear wall to exhaust at its peak. To date, the clients have never felt any need for fans or airconditioners.

The house is planned over three levels. The lower level contains the children's bedroom and play area, laundry, sauna and large covered deck abutting the wall of the swimming pool. In here we have placed two glass portholes to admit light to the lower areas and provide views back into the swimming pool.

The main level contains all the necessary living, entry and recreational functions, from swimming pool with decks overlooking the ocean, to garages opening to the kitchen. This area has a wonderful space and air flow rising through a void from the bedrooms below and across the double volume of the upper level. A simple, elegant stainless steel balustrade suspended walkway connects the main bedroom and guest bed/study at opposite ends of the building.

One of the client requirements was that the guest bed/study should have unobstructed views to the ocean. To achieve this and maintain ceiling heights to the living area, we raked the roof in two directions; first, towards the ocean to keep within the height limit, and then to the south so that the roof came below the finished level of the deck. The effect was striking and especially dramatic inside the living area. As the height limit reduced towards the south, we dropped the level of the floor to the music room to accommodate it.

On the living room deck we positioned the swimming pool partially under the main bedroom. We have found over the years that in the hot summer days the water can become uncomfortably warm and this partial shade is a decided advantage. The house is constructed of basically concrete masonry with polished timber floors, plasterboard linings and corrugated steel roof.

The kitchen was designed and fabricated in Germany by friends of the clients who then travelled with it to Australia and installed it in the house. Renate is extremely talented and her clean classic handling of the spaces delights the eye. It is my pleasure when, between trips, I am invited to share a cup of the best coffee and her wonderful cakes with her and David. The pleasures of architecture can live on well after completion of the contract.

Right Voids contribute to efficient air circulation that makes airconditioning redundant.

Opposite The main bedroom straddles the pool deck. Vertical slot louvred windows facilitate ventilation.

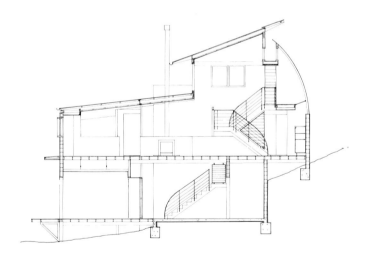

Opposite The west-facing
rear reflects the telescoped
nature of the site.

Right and below
Main bedroom above the
pool deck provides partial
shade to maintain a cooler
summer water temperature.

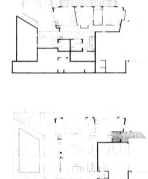

Opposite Kitchen and
living rooms reflect
the utilitarian edge of sleek
modernity. While the 'look'
is decidedly 'high-tech',
the house is in reality one
of fine simplicity.
Raked ceilings contribute
to unobstructed views.

Right The thinness
and fineness of the form
is exemplified by the
stainless steel staircase.
Note the angled toughened
glass strip along the rear
wall to provide additional
ambient lighting.

Alkira Apartments Noosa Hill 1997

This building is the second attempt we had at this site. It had been bought by the client some years earlier, with approval to build up to ten units. The first design we created was for five to six units, but this did not proceed and the project was suspended. Several years later the client returned with a revised brief that called for three units only, with the top penthouse designed as the client's retirement accommodation.

This time the client's wife said, 'Now, you keep out of it, Wally, and let Gabriel have a good go at it.' Wally said, 'Well, that's OK, so long as he doesn't give me another one of his bloody chook houses.' The design grew from a close collaboration between all three of us.

The building, set on Noosa Hill, commands magnificent views over Hastings Street, the Noosa River, and north up the beach to Double Island Point. The design for the building incorporated two luxury units, complete with private swimming pools, to be sold off on completion. The client's own unit was the real purpose for constructing the complex, and this was set to the rear and higher end of the site, thus maximising view and aspect. Two large hoop pine trees, which for years had been a Noosa landmark, were nurtured and retained as part of the overall design.

The penthouse was then designed, with its own lift over three floors. The lowest floor, at entry level, comprised lobby and stair, two guest bedrooms with bathroom, and laundry space. The next level contained the main living and recreation spaces. A library/study with built-in fireplace and attached bathroom at the rear was also designed as extra guest bed space. The main living room opened, through a disappearing glass wall, to the north, on to a wide balcony with views as far as the eye can see.

To the west, the kitchen was dropped 1.2 metres below the living room level. This removed it as an obstruction to the view, but also avoided the necessity of providing ugly pool fencing, by raising the pool outside the kitchen to living room floor level and providing the 1.2 metre step-up required by law. The effect was for the living room to provide a spectacular vista across the swimming pool to the wonderful unobstructed view of Noosa River and the mountains beyond.

The master bedroom with ensuite was situated on the top level and overlooks an atrium above the living area. Glazed on three sides and with a glass balustrade to the sleeping area, the extensive and beautiful views were maintained.

Materials were kept simple, but fittings and floor finishes are luxurious and a nautical seaside character was retained throughout the unit. The building was designed to ventilate without the necessity for ceiling fans or airconditioning. However, due to the proximity of the Reef Hotel and the main road outside, it is necessary to close the building up at night for sound insulation and this necessitates the inclusion of airconditioning.

The curved staircase to the master bedroom was housed in semi-circular zinc steel cladding, and was Wally's one concession to my propensity for chook houses.

Below and opposite
The Alkira penthouse exudes a nautical architecture that suggests more than a passing reference to ocean liners.

Opposite The main
living area is capped
by a clerestory lantern,
and the main north-facing
wall of glass fully retracts
to capture air movement
and provide an expanded
entertaining area.

Right The master
bedroom and ensuite
overlooks an atrium above
the living area, as well
as panoramic views over
Hastings Street, Noosa
River and north to Double
Island Point.

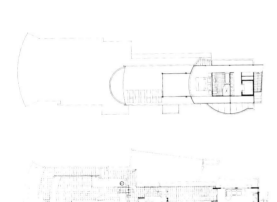

Prell Residence Sunshine Beach 1997

Gabriel and Christina came to me prior to their marriage on the recommendation of a friend of theirs and were warned that I did not do the type of architecture they desired and would probably not accept the brief. Our meeting generated an immediate warmth and they found true respect for my work. As Christina said, 'We loved Gabriel and Elizabeth as people. We loved their work. He has the reputation of being a good architect, so why can't he design the type of house we require?' And so a close friendship, and wonderful working relationship, was formed.

I guided them away from conventional thinking of Mediterranean architecture, towards the philosophy of Barragan and Legoretta, but with its own connotations to site and environment. I persuaded them to dispense with main balconies to the view, as these faced prevailing winds and were unlikely to be of much use. Instead, I offered a large central courtyard set into the side of the hill and sheltered from the worst of the weather, but looking through generous windows of the living room to the ocean beyond.

The plan entailed two, two-storey pavilions stepping down the hill, the lower for living and car parking and the other for sleeping, guest rooms and laundry. The transition between the pavilions was by covered way and stairs protected by canvas awnings. As with Lake Weyba, the decision was taken to provide a plunge pool rather than a full-size swimming pool, and this was located on the terrace outside the main bedroom, and would become a later play pool for future children.

The building was constructed from concrete block to create the large projections and recesses around openings, to form weather protection and a form of false eaves. Aluminium-framed windows were placed in strongly stated timber frames, and care was taken to ensure the rooms were afforded the same quality of ventilation that we built into our more lightweight structures. Strongly stated spitters were built into the gutter systems to avoid flooding in heavy rains. The house is a delight to walk into and experience — a feeling enhanced by its owners.

Below and opposite

Poole's Mexican/ Mediterranean style is an unusual break from his lighter structural solutions.

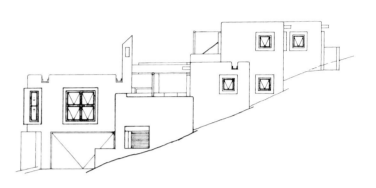

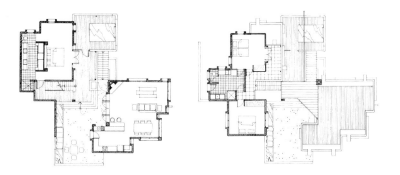

Opposite Site driven,
the house is broken up
into a series of connected
modules. Although of solid
mass, the principles of
natural ventilation are
extensively incorporated.

Right Rooftop and
courtyards satisfy
the architect's
preoccupation with
comfort zone options.

Grant Residence Sunshine Beach 1997

Roger and Cheryl Grant had, for some years, been taking their holidays in a house I designed years ago at Sunshine Beach. When the block next door to their holiday house came up for sale, they bought it and commissioned me to design their new house. Built on the north face of the steep edge of a gully running into the ocean, the house is nestled behind the hill and is well sheltered from undesirable and prevailing south-easterly winds and weather.

This house was to be strongly disciplined by the council's planning restrictions that imposed a 9 metre height limit. Because of the heavy coastal scrub, it was necessary to elevate the house to a minimum height to optimise views. The house became squashed between the necessary floor height and the maximum allowable building height. Sea views from the house were also restricted to east and west. To maximise the aspects, we took a point of reference in front of the building and planned the building in arcs from the point so that every position in the house would obtain ocean views.

Because of the inclined site, roof angle and height limit, we were not able to project the roof over the northern deck for sun protection because of head height. The decision was taken to create large battened shutters with shade cloth linings. These hinged over the glass face to provide additional storm protection, and could be raised by means of gas struts to a position that shaded the northern deck. In this temporary position, they exceeded the height limit.

Similarly, the ceiling inside the house over the living room and in front of the mezzanine main bedroom was considered oppressive. We decided to hinge a whole section of the roof to relieve the oppression, to let in the sky, the view and a cross-flow of air. Working with the fabricators and hydraulics engineer, we discovered that by installing large rams, we could lift the roof with mains water pressure from the town water supply and another innovation was born.

The western side of the house also required ventilation, as well as privacy from the adjoining house. We achieved this by providing batten and shade cloth openings to western walls and hinging over them translucent panels operated with ropes and gas struts. In the open position these panels shaded the western wall, opened up the eastern wall to light and ventilation, and provided privacy from the neighbours. There is a beautiful flow of air and space through this building. It has the relaxed air and fun of a true beach holiday house.

Below Surrounded by a quirky combination of neighbours, the house exhibits a wedged-shape roof and cranked plan to maximise the orientation and difficult site.

Opposite Fully adjustable lightweight external screens and a roof opening which is operated hydraulically by water pressure are some of the keys to flexible design.

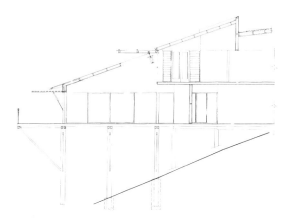

Below The lightweight roof section opens to expel heat and provide superb beach views from the top-floor master bedroom.

Right and opposite
An inclined site, roof angle and height limit thwarted Poole's ability to project the structure across the northern deck. Instead, he provided battened, shade-cloth shutters on gas struts. Views are to Sunshine Beach.

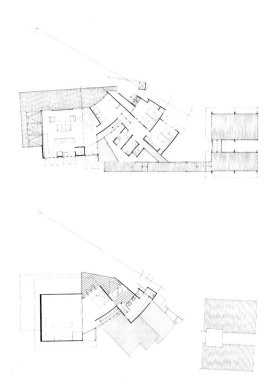

Capricorn 151 Display Home Coolum 1997

It has always been my claim and desire that architecture is part of my purpose and that part of my existence is to take architecture to the people. One way of achieving this is by affordable project housing. We now seem to have put together a team and product which may make some very small dent on the Australian mass housing market and the Australian consciousness.

These designs have been carefully and thoroughly developed with the cooperation of all parties. The special component here has been the time, patience and quality of the effort and engineering ability injected into the project by Rod Bligh of Bligh Tanner. Engineers have generally found it difficult to deal with my brand of madness. Rod is one of those who has managed.

The system is based on a strict grid and simple, lightweight steel portals, pre-nailed wall frames and simple, off-the-shelf materials. The old bushman's breezeway has been rediscovered and put to use through the ability to secure it with garage doors at both ends. Ventilation through the houses has been carefully and thoroughly considered, and the invention of the in-wall pivoting vent met my requirement that all corners of all rooms to any house should be cross-ventilated.

Links have been designed so that houses can be constructed of connected pavilions, with service areas or breezeways to create buildings of varying shapes and sizes to accommodate the needs of families. We are presently extending the system to include the maligned brick veneer house. It is probably a preferred building type by our communities, and as architects we should be able to turn it into a more attractive and livable article, which may just enhance the quality of people's lives.

Opposite Even a simple concept such as the Capricorn 151 incorporates the luxury of a central breezeway to provide comfortable privacy and prospect. A broad skylight ensures soft illumination.

Opposite below A linear, narrow-waisted composition of low thermal mass allows for rapid cooling. Turbine ventilators and lightweight cladding combine with internal 'gills' to provide efficient air flow.

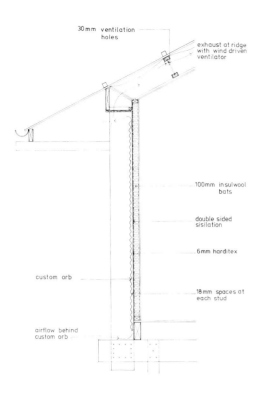

30mm ventilation
holes

exhaust at ridge
with wind driven
ventilator

100mm insulwool
bats

double sided
sisilation

6mm harditex

custom orb

18mm spaces at
each stud

airflow behind
custom orb

Below The main living
area expands into the
central deck which
provides a buffer from
sleeping quarters.

Opposite
Breezeway skylight.

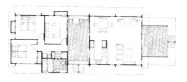

From Dylan —
the music of architecture

"My architecture is frequently portrayed as unconventional, and I would like to believe that is true in the way I go about arriving at solutions ... Knowing how to remain open to influences but to identify and reject fashions, how to remain receptive and sensitive to the possibilities, yet not be overwhelmed by dross, is foremost to me."

John Mainwaring

Some of my earliest influences remain among the most important. Besides such studies as Japanese architecture and Taliesen West, my architecture was inspired in the late 1960s and 1970s by Bob Dylan, Jack Kerouac and others who symbolised a free spirit which captured the mood of the era. They helped form my philosophy and desire to ward off what I would term architecture's 'comfort zone'. I have since taken the view that good architecture should challenge everything that has gone before and looks for refinement and improvement, even if it is in subtle and incremental steps.

My architecture is frequently portrayed as unconventional, and I would like to believe that is true in the way I go about arriving at solutions. It is one of life's constant challenges to discover the 'real' person inside and have this reflected in your body of work. Knowing how to remain open to influences but to identify and reject fashions, how to remain receptive and sensitive to the possibilities, yet not be overwhelmed by dross, is foremost to me.

It is a rule I apply to my own work as a way of taking the next step forward. Architecture can provide the same joy and stimulation as great music. We just have to understand how to make the journey. There is still plenty of the alternative element in my work. By that I don't mean Bob Marley reggae, frayed edges and casually made.

I am especially interested in why Australian culture finds it hard to come to terms with the patina and ageing of materials within buildings. How do we create places that bring meaning and joy? We have a fear of letting buildings, environments and people grow old gracefully. Why should design be anything less than inspirational or aspirational with a respect for the user?

I don't believe any of my work is esoteric or elite, so much as responsive to the place or community for which it is designed. Hopefully it invites questions, makes pertinent comment and introduces humour in a time when our culture appears brittle and overwhelmed by imported styles. Sociopolitical issues, the environment and conservation are very much in the forefront of my work. When Australians wander away from their non-pretentious, utilitarian and disciplined beginnings, they inevitably fall victim to Robin Boyd's 'Australian Ugliness'.

Right and below A flair for structural reduction and edges that wafer is evident at Mountview guest quarters and (bottom) Mainwaring's own house.

Opposite Mainwaring's architecture relies heavily on 'edges' and 'openings'. His design for the Jones Residence on Noosa Waters (1997) highlights the importance of landscape over status symbols.

My ideas not only reflect who I am and how I see the world, but they also reflect the kind of clients I attract. Many people imagine the Sunshine Coast as the heartland of hedonistic youth. The reality is that it has a high proportion of the elderly. The St Vincent's Nursing Home, completed in 1997, is a good example. It incorporates many of the solutions evolved as a response to place. This project is the antithesis of the deadening institutional solution. It contributes to the region's built environment and urban philosophy. The brief demanded security for patients, yet we had to provide for dignity without simply applying it, as so often happens, as some sort of buzz word.

One of the approaches I share with Gabriel, Lindsay and Kerry is a commitment to local trades and craftspeople. These services and supplies form part of a regional approach to design and problem-solving which makes the architectural 'package' fully integrated. Instead of importing furniture, fittings and fixtures, we have involved local people who better understand the direction and requirements of our architecture.

By nurturing a team of cabinet-makers, metal-workers, carpenters and fabricators, we have helped develop an infrastructure finely tuned to the architecture.

There are many influences on my work, ranging from Australian and Pacific Rim vernacular to the raw reality of Third World squatter settlement. We live in a unique part of the world where architecture should be more about space, air and lightness. By 'lightness' we mean not just sitting lightly on the ground, but a cultural lightness whereby natural light and lightness embrace and contrast heaviness. Some of the projects in this book show examples of the abstracted idea of the verandah house with long thin plans so conducive to cross-ventilation and natural light. These are principally expressed in the form of H, U, I and L floor plan configurations.

All of it has taught me to keep questioning the nature of what I do and why I do it. There are times when architecture can bring on depression and moments of elation, but I still believe in the capacity for joyful surprise. Hopefully, I can still pleasantly surprise the unsuspecting punter.

Opposite Framed by a specimen jacaranda, the Mountview residence at Kenilworth dissolves at the edges in the best tree-house tradition.

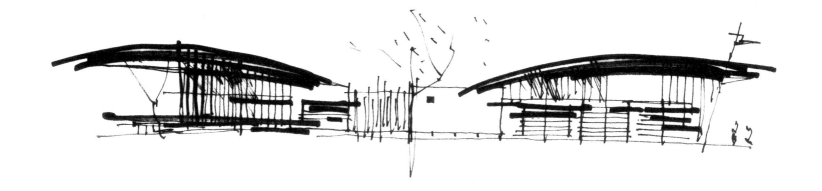

Opposite and below
The University of the
Sunshine Coast Library
and Jones Residence
clerestory detail (top) typify
Mainwaring's consistent
resolution.

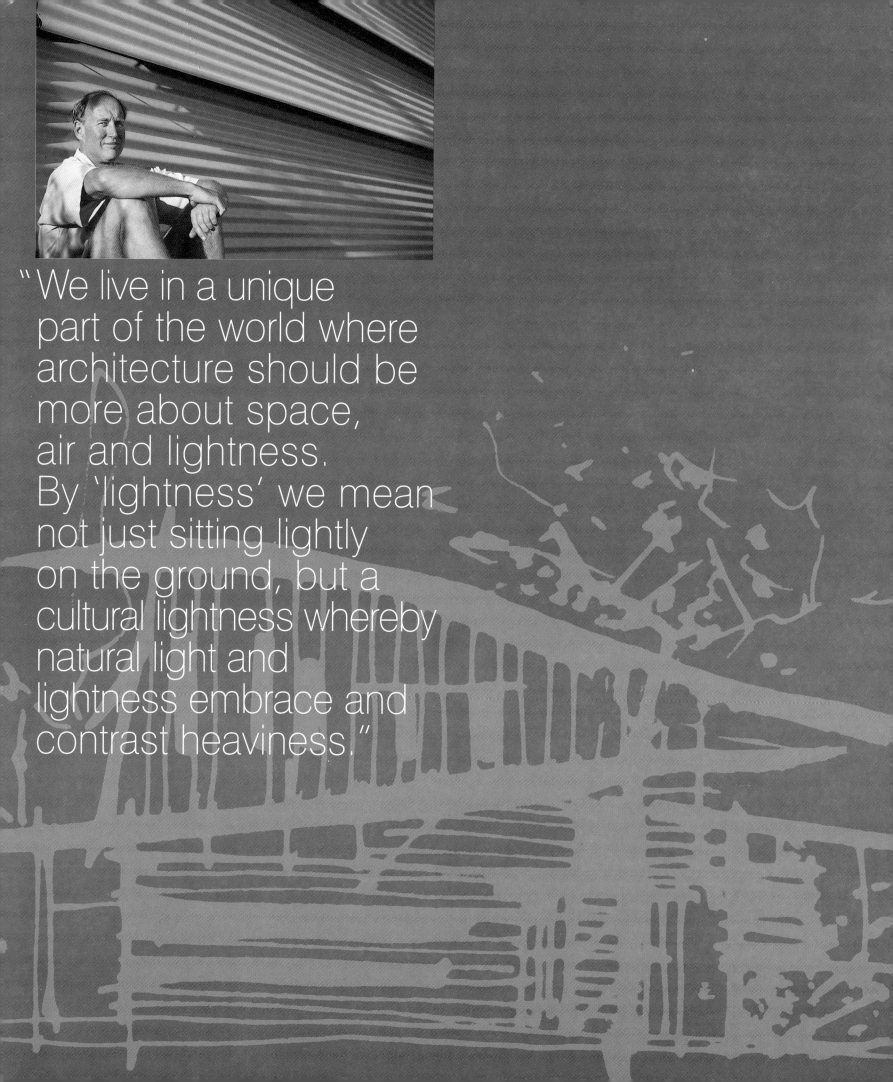

"We live in a unique
part of the world where
architecture should be
more about space,
air and lightness.
By 'lightness' we mean
not just sitting lightly
on the ground, but a
cultural lightness whereby
natural light and
lightness embrace and
contrast heaviness."

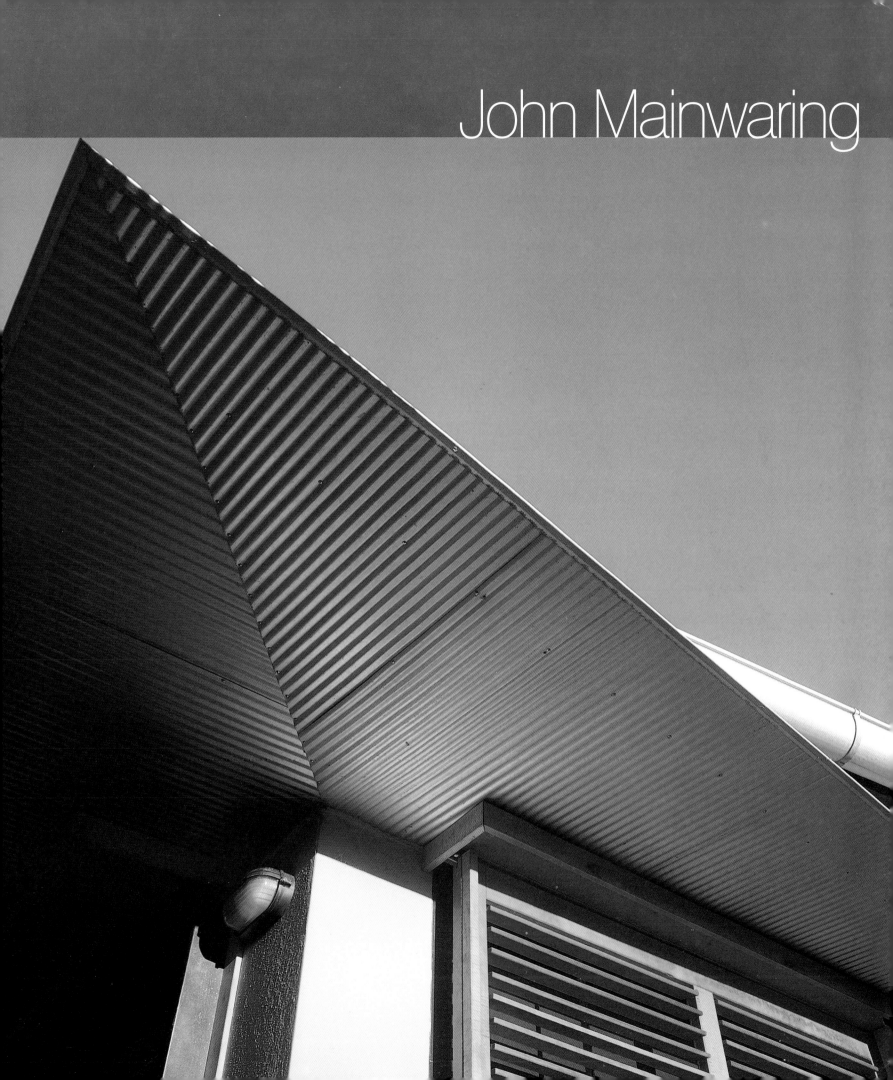

Richardson House Noosa Hill 1987

This hill-top residence was planned to carefully integrate with its generous allotment and bushland setting of perfumed gum trees and banksias. The house has an organic, informal quality based around an L-shaped plan. Various projections and decks cantilever to make a vivid connection with the immediate bush and, on the uppermost levels, provide superb 360-degree views across the adjacent national park, south towards Sunshine Beach and west across the Noosa River and hinterland.

A clear hierarchy of spaces occurs within the context of a timber-clad structure on steel stilts which allows instant 'gardens' outside all living areas and bedrooms. The bush setting provides great privacy and outlook and invites an architecture of sensitivity to relate to its surroundings. The residence makes minimum physical intrusion, but has a high visual and aesthetic impact that treats the skyline and ecosystem as a priority.

Living areas are predominantly located in the tower section which faces east towards the Pacific Ocean, while bedrooms located over two levels comprise the north section of the house. The slender, curved steel roof form of the sleeping quarters and carport is an early motif that echoes earlier experience with Gabriel Poole on The Hastings in downtown Noosa Heads. The project is typified by simple, bold detailing with an emphasis on providing maximum function and performance for minimum cost.

A simple island kitchen bench provides an organisational focus on the top level. The kitchen/dining-room open plan and island bench, with modest materials well used, provide a planned, but informal, organisation of space. Windows can be opened and angled on all six sides of the tower to catch prevailing breezes, while the Venturi's thermal exhaust action is facilitated by the vertical corridor of the tower to provide a climate-sensitive response.

Below and opposite

High on Noosa Hill, on the cusp of a national park, the house twists from the plan at the tower to assume optimum orientation and views.

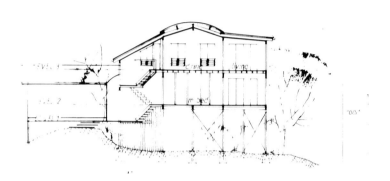

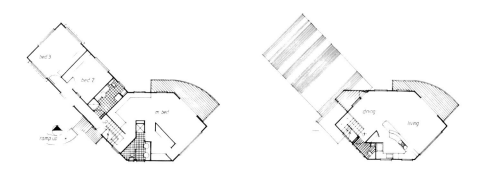

Opposite Two decks
cantilever from the
two-floor living room
and kitchen to optimise
the internal/external
experience.

Right A lower-level
bedroom and carport
are housed beneath the
vaulted lightweight roof.

Powell House Noosa River 1991

This south-east Queensland detached town house takes full advantage of wonderful light and cross-ventilation opportunities in this region. The H-shaped plan consists of two long, thin 'wings' with an atrium or breezeway in the middle that provides a private garden courtyard. A series of transitional courtyard spaces lead from a central connecting foyer to a busy arterial road on one side, while living spaces overlook the Noosa River.

The introverted nature of this concept embodies an east wing or 'long house' that contains all of the living activities — laundry, kitchen, dining and deck — in a simple linear progression. It has open-plan flexibility for different types of indoor and outdoor entertaining. The kitchen island bars and table, for instance, can be used for serving sushi, breakfast, cocktails or conventional dining.

The western wing comprises bedrooms on both levels, with an ensuite to the master bedroom on the first floor. The master bedroom with deck overlooks the river and features sliding timber shutters for privacy and north-west sun control. As this deck returns into the central atrium, privacy is provided by the high skillion roof over the living space in the east wing.

Living and dining areas resemble the enclosed Queensland verandah, an idiom used by a number of innovative architects in the region. These 'thin' buildings have extra walls and windows at additional cost, but provide a natural form of passive airconditioning. Breezes pass through vegetation in the atrium and the whole house consists of a series of interconnecting 'verandahs'.

External ply wall cladding is lightly stained maroon and turquoise. This is influenced by early timber houses and by the colour depth of the river. Other materials include a corrugated steel roof and lime wash render. The house still contains images of the traditional Queensland vernacular boatshed, and other influences include a pre-1900 vernacular coffee plantation homestead by Buderim pioneer Harry Board. Contrary to the typical colonial house plans of the period, this house contained narrow living wings with a central landscaped space.

Interior colours and textures reflect water, beach environment and river, and contrast the rich jarrah and silky oak joinery and windows. Especially made large 'droopy' timber fan blades, timber venetians and shutters give diffused light patterns and privacy. Casement windows can be angled into the atrium to draw in the cooling north-east sea breeze. Stainless steel fittings contrast the timber floor and joinery. Because the central landscaped atrium is private, this south-east Queensland design concept is well suited to high urban density and allows immediate living spaces to be fully exploited.

Opposite An architecture of great composition. The outlook is exquisitely framed by casement windows.

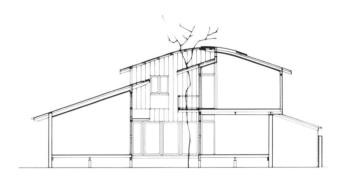

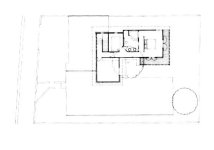

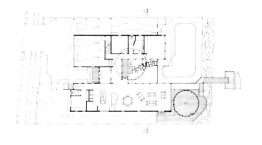

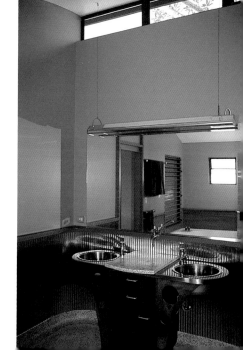

Opposite Kitchen and
dining areas benefit
from appropriately used
lightweight materials that
subtly reinforce the
aesthetic of crafted utility.

Right With a north-facing
Noosa River frontage,
the Powell House is the
antithesis of the riverfront
mansion. Frayed with
louvres, blinds and
weathered timbers,
the project reinterprets
the pre-1900 coffee
plantation vernacular.

Canal House Noosa Waters 1993

This stark, discordant, utilitarian house creates a fascinating dichotomy with its neighbours. It is provocative and mildly subversive in a sea of terracotta and speculative housing. Neighbours disparagingly refer to it as 'the woolshed', for the very reason that it expresses materials honestly and without deception. The woolshed metaphor is discordant because the house is much closer to an urban rocket or arrowhead. It is explicit about being contemporary and expresses a strong cultural connotation.

Good Australian design has its roots in utility and ignores the imported pastiche that turns its back on climate, orientation and outlook. This is a house of difference. It clearly contrasts with its neighbours, which have created a Jurassic Park all of their own. It is designed to survive the buffeting from neighbouring 'monsters' and, in many ways, this contrast helps the house to become stronger. Its thin, slender envelope reveals another way of responding to place and exposes some of the flaws inherent in ponderous, transplanted design.

In response, the western wall corners of the house have been glazed against what would appear to be appropriate sun control practices, but experience suggests natural illumination can be effectively provided even from narrow cavity sites. In this instance a transparent timber slotted ceiling and windows permit a soft wash of natural illumination and, by night, is heaven for star-gazers. One of the boundary outbuildings, the boatport, doubles to become a second meals preparation area and is perfect for the outdoor chargrill, making kitchen maintenance much easier.

On the north side of the house a retractable glass wall has been placed on a 25-degree slant to face true north-east. This allows true indoor/outdoor living. It also permits cross-ventilation when there is wind from both the north and the south. Fully retractable and adjustable shutters provide filtered privacy to the canal. The whole layout is open plan with a large mezzanine studio and ensuite. Living spaces downstairs are extroverted with adjustable privacy screening. Upstairs is less flexible and more introverted with glimpses, rather than vistas, of water, to maintain privacy without curtains.

As covenants do not allow vertical wall or sheet steel walls, the mute western wall is angled at 15 degrees to become a covenant-approved roof or 'woof' — half wall, half roof. When local real estate agents drive by, the faint chanting of 'woof, woof' can be heard. It may be coincidental, but it usually coincides with the southerly that whistles through the garage's corrugated 'gills' and funnels air through the house in Venturi fashion.

Right The layered west-facing wall/roof, or 'woof', provides privacy from neighbours yet permits ample natural light through a series of screens and slots.

Opposite Winner of the prestigious Robin Boyd Award for residential design (1995), Mainwaring attempts to satisfy the most critical client of all — the architect.

Left A soaring, double height volume is further articulated by the skeletal structure and given visual warmth of ply cladding.

Opposite Suburbia is challenged by a building of uncompromised elegance.

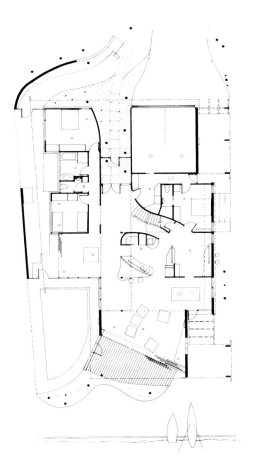

Left Nautical but not trite or cliched in the process. Fins, blades, portal windows on the facing (west) wall and battened cement sheet ceilings prove that quality is a state of mind, not necessarily huge budgets.

Right and below
Light and shade are predominant themes. The thin, sinuous roofline is repeated in all internal structural details and treatments. The result is an interior that mirrors the exterior profile.

Chapman Residence Noosaville 1994

In the early 1980s, one of the local identities was a Coolum surfer named Grommet. During a 'big night out' with his mates, Grommet went to Brisbane and stayed at the Breakfast Creek Hotel. The hotel caught fire and Grommet died in the blaze. In many ways, his demise represents the loss of an original character and was a warning of things to come. Amid an emerging built culture of treacle-like render and pseudo-Doric columns, the old, unpretentious fibro cement-clad shop of the 1950s has been flattened. Its wonderful simplicity, lightness, cove-striped cladding and ribbon casement fenestration has been replaced by so-called taste-conscious 'brick-veneerial' and bullnose building.

The Chapman house provided the opportunity to connect once again with the simple values from Grommet's era of the corner shop. It epitomises simple, lightweight materials and an imagery of improvisation and quality resourcefulness. Contrasting this are the contemporary methods of fenestration, retractable walls, timber louvres, vent louvres and adjustable transparency.

The residence is a continuation of the evolutionary design, developing light and cross-ventilation of the so-called thin, or narrow-waisted, verandah house. With the north-east aspect contradicting the vista, this interesting design twist developed. The toe of the L-shaped plan needed degrees of transparency in its outer walls, and adjustable transparency was obtained with retractable glass walls and stack-back timber louvre panels. Conceptually the house comprises longitudinal zones of transparency.

As the site is long and thin, there is a small journey from the garage and road to arrive at the living area. The whole block of land acts as an extension of the building footprint. The robust red rock base provides privacy, as well as assisting acoustic and security issues for the lightweight articulated upper storey. The L-shaped plan acts as a protector to the south-east, yet allows flexibility for views to the north and the environment park to the south. All rooms in the single-cell, linear plan have access to northerly courts using 'non-walls' and adjustable fenestration.

The 'L' comprises a number of living cells including au pair room, laundry and guest quarters that culminates in a guest tower that addresses the street. The master bedroom zone is a retreat with ensuite, study and comfortable walk-in robes. The entire upstairs space forms a mezzanine over the entrance corridor and provides a sense of spatial comfort in this narrow vertical zone. Reverse-angle timber louvres in the north wall allow parents to observe swimming pool activity. This reverse-wall fenestration accentuates the internal/external relationship from the courtyard and provides a key transition zone. Views through this upper-level fenestration reveal layered ply ceiling planes.

In addition to retractable fenestration, banks of louvres and extended, thin ribbon windows, sand-blasted glass is used with internal venetian blinds to provide almost infinite control of vistas and privacy. With its multiple references and layers, the house provides a juxtaposition of functions expressed as towers and protrusions. Grommet's slatted, fibro-cement sheet is there, along with timber screens and zinc-coated mini orb. All this sits on a sponged, lime-washed masonry base to produce the lightweight top sitting on an aged rock base.

Below A pandanus palm frames the L-shaped north face.

Opposite The embodiment of architecture as an envelope. Traditional status building materials are cast aside in favour of kiosk vernacular. Compressed cement sheet provides the binding element in this residence of 'improvised' flair.

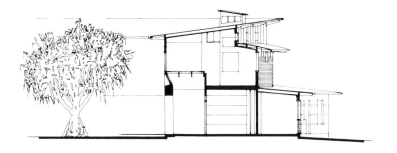

Below The plywood balustrade reveals the relationship of seeing 'through' things rather than simply looking 'at' things.

Opposite top
A heightened sense of layers and screens in the top-floor master bedroom.

Opposite below
Noosa River to the left (south) and courtyard to the right provide an option of 'open' and 'closed' environments.

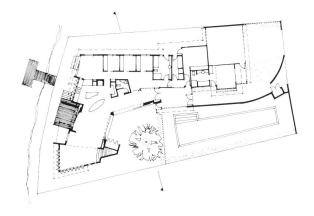

Mountview Residence Kenilworth 1996

Based around an 1890 timber homestead and dairy farm, the property now belongs to a German baron and his Australian-born wife. Sited on a delightful ridge, the project is ringed by bunya pines, an endemic species sacred to Aboriginal pre-white history.

This triumvirate of structures — residence, guest house and restored pioneer's cottage — form a special linkage with their environment in the hinterland of the Sunshine Coast. The termite-riddled 'Queenslander' was saved and bridged by a breezeway to a contemporary, two-storey shed. The third structure, a guest pavilion, is located some 40 metres to the east to create a rural colonnade. The three buildings form a crescent shape and are connected with timber walkways.

In the existing homestead, the roof rafter system is expressed and supports a yacht cabin-style ceiling of Queensland pine. The new architectural work is extroverted, airy and opens up new vistas. The old chook shed provided a more relevant reference than the homestead, which was designed under a protective phobia of security from the perceived harsh climate, bushrangers, Aboriginal tribes and the ever-present bunyip!

The project was a complex one of salvaging the old homestead riddled with white-ant. By re-stumping, re-roofing and inserting a structural steel frame and bracing, the building was rescued from a state of near demolition. Spare knife-edge steelwork provides structural bracing and a vigorous counterpoint to the old mellowed timbers. Its once boxy enclosure is now a light-filled, flexible, open plan easily divided by sliding 'shoji' screens made from recycled timbers. The design interprets the old spirit, yet injects it with a contemporary reading of classical and contemporary influences.

The second building connects with the old house by a bridge walled only with fly wire. Upstairs the new sections comprise master bedroom, kitchen and deck. Downstairs are an outdoor room, laundry, spa room and garage. The south-western wall is expressed as a simple corrugated wave and is the antithesis of the rigid geometry of the original homestead. This wall simply 'dags off' with its frayed, lightly jagged, corrugated steel edge. Materials that evoke the owners' passion for sailing and a building of contemporary form are typified by the extensive use of cabin ply throughout.

The guest house comprises two pavilions connected by a bridge. This opens up to become a breezeway in summer and closes to become a solarium in winter. Its silver corrugated steel envelope produces a thermally efficient environment, while the butterfly roof shape allows for highly effective ventilation. Glass louvres with venetians above the door extract warm air, while in winter, the clerestory created by the roof acts as a solar absorber.

Below The overhauled 1890s' 'Queenslander' homestead (right) is unambiguously contrasted by the new house which, while contemporary, is sympathetic to the materiality and spirit of the original.

Opposite The breezeway between the old homestead and new incorporates a papaya tree.

Below View through 'old' homestead along breezeway. Skilful restoration avoided demolition of the pioneer's cottage.

Right and opposite
A sweeping corrugated steel wall frays to a distinctively sculptural edge.

Right Utilitarian materials
and detailing provide
function and 'style'.

Below The connection
between kitchen and
verandah is exemplary.
Note the arched roof
truss and ply ceiling.

Opposite A beach kiosk
aesthetic is employed
for an informal,
yet rigorous solution.

Wright House Noosa Hinterland 1997

This house marks its territory with great sensitivity. A slashing diagonal roof on this pavilion residence accentuates the site and respects the verdant backdrop. From the street elevation the house flows with the fall line of the steep site. The thin steel roof reads as a blade or flowing pencil line scribed through the air. This slenderness of materials is carried through with compressed fibrous cement sheet and timbers featured extensively inside and out.

Presented as a series of thin edges, the house can be viewed as easily as the pages of an open book. Rather than a single skin or resolute box, the design is attenuated and animated by awnings, louvres and screens. These, however, are never arbitrary or add-ons in the vein of speculative housing riddled with throw-away references to an imagined subtropical environment. A thinness of edge is translated throughout the body of the house, which is narrow enough to engage its site with a great degree of intimacy. Topography provides the design driver, as does rainwater runoff, collection and storage.

The house is built over four levels and connected by three staircases. This provides generous space while making easy visual linkages. On the top floor are the main bedroom, ensuite and broad deck. The main living level comprises the kitchen, dining and family room. On the level beneath are two bedrooms, and further down is the garage. Vertical and horizontal slatted screens are used extensively inside and out to filter the views and the light. Generous deck areas encourage an improved relationship with the sublime climate. This is further extended into the landscape where a series of courtyards and vegetable and herb gardens capture the essence of the clients' affinity with this place.

While there is a specific hierarchy of zones and spatial organisation, the feel is deliberately loose and informal. Internally, materials are expressed simply and honestly — a combination of lightly stained timbers, compressed fibre cement sheet and galvanised steelwork. Externally, materials are juxtaposed to achieve a nautical feel of slender function requiring complete environmental response and flexibility.

Below and opposite
A slashing diagonal roofline signals a convincing originality. It reflects a sensitivity to site, being considerate of the views of neighbours. On the east side, however, the house reverses its streetside privacy to embrace the panorama.

Over page The slenderness of the house is echoed by the thinness of materials. Corrugated steel and compressed cement sheet successfully resist popular notions of 'prestige' cladding and finishes.

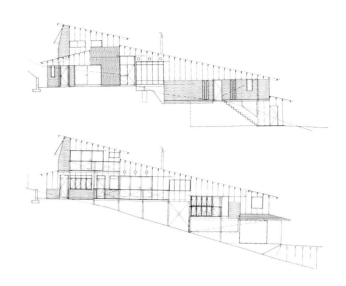

Left and opposite
The house relates to the utilitarian hinterland lodge building stock which expresses its form and material usage. Simple tectonics owe a debt to Finnish architecture. Interiors are elegant but refrain from the highly modish.

University of the Sunshine Coast Library
Sippy Downs 1997

This is an exploration of what can be done to make a climate-responsive building visually stimulating and a pleasure to experience. A library should symbolise achievement, aspiration and curiosity. These are qualities Lawrence Nield and I have tried to ensure are central to the concept of the USC library. In many respects the building resembles a beautiful big bird. It is of necessity sleek and highly functional, but it also feathers. It is not a box of clearly defined edges that specifies what students must and must not do. It is implicit that the building belongs to students and teaching staff and is highly flexible.

The formalism of the Jefferson-inspired master plan for Virginia University did not restrict us to a narrow interpretation of classical architecture. We preferred to contrast that formal part and celebrate the difference of place using vernacular materials in a high-spirited, inventive way. It was intended that the library formed a solid anchor to the existing neoclassical wings or urban elements. Instead, we produced a verandah structure that allows views to read through. Instead of images from antiquity, our references included the great woolstores of Sydney and Brisbane with their warehousing capacity and sawtooth top lighting. This led to the climatic and organisational reference and this is most evident in the top floor — reading and study areas — which was where wool was given microscopic examination. Just as the great warehouses used the lower floors for storage, so too the library compresses storage, processing and computers on the lower and mid-levels.

Once again it falls within the category as a building of loose fit, but there is an underlying discipline to ensure that the level of spatial arrangement and construction is of a high order. The roof, or rather roofs, feather and brush lightly against the sky and provide a strong first impression of difference. The library is reached by stairs (or lift) on the north-western face and lends a sense of importance or ceremony to the process of higher education. The elevation also helps to catch prevailing breezes for those who just wish to sit. It also improves vistas from all levels.

Bristling skillion roofs provide multiple openings for natural light and echo the great slatted verandah on the north. We went to great effort to provide high-quality detailing, such as the outrigger columns of the verandah. This involved much more than structural decoration. It contributes to the quality of space stripped bare, yet is enriched with setbacks, undercrofts, courtyards, verandahs, and various places of assembly inside and out. As good as it looks, this is as much a building to actually use and enjoy as, hopefully, to admire.

Right and below
An elevated verandah provides a popular vantage point and meeting place. Built-in seating reflects a genuine interest in user function and satisfaction.

Opposite A bristling skillion roof flares rhythmically to generate an architecture of understated force and simplicity.

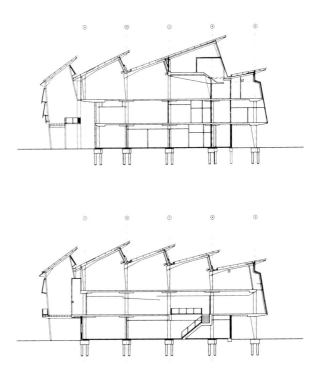

Opposite top and right

Elegant verandah detailing
to outrigger columns
produces a distinctive
sailing metaphor.

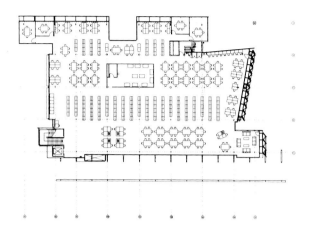

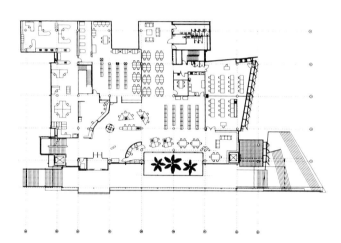

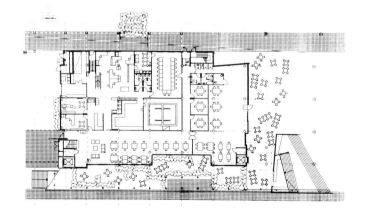

Right An elliptical
suspended ceiling provides
a playful gesture at reception.

Below Blade columns
in the top floor library are
reminders of the industrial
aesthetic which drives the
structure.

Opposite Roaming
kangaroos on campus
are reminders of the fragile
encounter of nature and
development.

St Vincent's Aged Care Nursing Home
Noosa Heads 1997

The design approach consciously rejected the notion of attempting to recreate an environment from the past by using kitsch colonial or federation references, the imagery of which is always dubious. Rather, we have abstractly designed an environment that provides comfort, warmth and reminders of the past while remaining modern and optimistic. This positive approach uses a palette of light, shade, space, tactile materials and colours evocative of 'coastal architecture' developing in the Noosa region.

A major challenge was to reconcile the client's requirements for a large-scale facility with the need to provide a legible, human-scale environment for residents. This was especially true of the dementia ward, which requires patients to be monitored in a secured area and thus is traditionally claustrophobic.

Set within a national park, it conveys a resort-style ambience instead of the bleak, institutional facility we have come to expect. This has translated into improved staff and visitor morale which directly affects the care given in a positive way. Variation in form, structure and materials without fake gables, etc, gives the building its character and village atmosphere, acknowledging it as an understated part of a (sub)urban background as opposed to a town monument or icon.

Stage one of the aged care facility for St Vincent's Community Services comprises an administration building designed to service the whole future complex, linking the nursing and special care wings. Stage one has thirty beds in the nursing wing and twenty beds in the dementia or special care wing. Later stages will provide a total capacity of up to 120 beds.

Natural light and different vistas to new and existing landscapes in conjunction with the layering of verandah zones provides further visual interest and stimulus. Cross-ventilation and passive airconditioning have been incorporated using transition verandah and courtyard spaces together with 'heat chimneys'. The fully insect-screened verandah spaces allow sleep, relaxation and living in true Australian style. With careful siting and expression, a real relationship is made with the neighbouring national park, with this small community informally being the custodians.

Above The modular nature of component parts resists the institutional style of so many facilities for the elderly.

Opposite top A design which successfully fuses architecture with landscape.

Opposite below A direct linkage to surrounding bushland is reinforced by the landscaped sanctuary of sheltered courtyards.

Below Few homes for the aged have a comparable quality of natural lighting.

Opposite Verandahs contribute to security without precluding communication or compromising vistas.

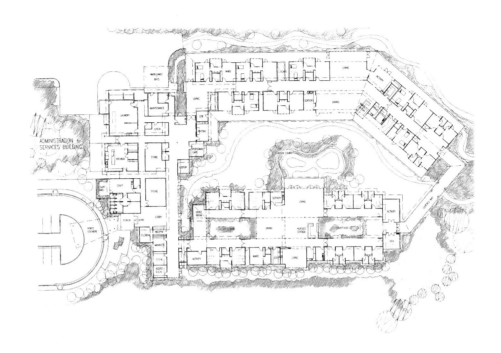

Seels House Sunshine Beach 1998

This tower house is an evolution of the Richardson house (1987), although the lower, horizontal component is a later stage. In our opinion, the original subdivision developer made a mistake and 'houselocked' this portion of the land so that it had no normal vistas or view lines on to streets, let alone the adjacent Noosa Heads National Park to the north.

One option was to produce a lower floor plan and create an introverted courtyard. This would have provided a very stuffy result with no possibility for cooling breezes. The periscope tower snags views over and in-between neighbours. This is also good for funnelling breezes into the house by placing the living room on the top floor and bedrooms on the lower level. Views are then possible from the kitchen, dining and living spaces.

The plan is essentially a triangle with a translucent U-shaped wall to the south and a glass point to the north of the lounge room on the top floor. This juxtaposes an elevated outdoor living area that 'floats' among the tree tops.

The deck comprises two sitting areas joined by a bridge. This configuration allows natural light to pass from the upstairs to downstairs bedrooms via light wells set in the deck through to the window below. Corrugated translucent wall slatting on the upper deck blocks neighbouring roofs and protects privacy while providing a 'cubby' house rooftop environment. External fibro cement sheeting has been cut into horizontal strips and eased out to resemble 'super' weatherboards. There are two-and-a-half bedrooms contained within the rectangular plan, with the half-room doubling as a TV nook and occasional bedroom/cupboard.

Right The twisted geometry of upper and lower levels facilitates optimum site usage with a minimal site footprint.

Opposite Transparent corrugated sheeting of south-facing alcove ensures indirect available light suffuses the central stairwell and body of the house.

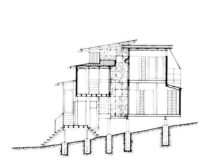

Right and below
The intersection
of overlapping cubes.

Opposite A lightweight
structural system requires
minimal excavation and
negligible impact on natural
drainage patterns.

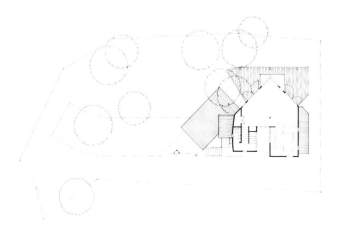

Timber Workshop, Hiller Residence
Kenilworth 1999

The Hiller workshop was designed as an adjunct pavilion to the Hiller residential 'rural village' (1996). The masonry base contains a store shed for farm machinery and a wine cellar. The latter caused this small 'post and beam' architectural practice some consternation because the brief called for the design of a brick barrel vault, which is foreign to the usual work carried out by our firm. Research revealed that the most efficient barrel arch incorporates the geometry of a sharper circle at the side as well as a larger circle for the top. The ground floor is washed gravel, as the client wanted no concrete to taint the environment in which rare wine is stored.

The roof line echoes the large curve running in two directions to create a reverse scissor-like roof with multiple clerestories. This permits ample southern light and northern winter light to suffuse a workshop where timber-laminating technology is being developed. As there is no ceiling, wool insulation has been detailed to sit neatly under the steel roof. The high-tech timber machinery shares pride of place with a freshwater crayfish-smoking oven.

The building's external single-skin cladding uses full 1.2 metre wide Ecoply as giant weatherboards, giving this small utilitarian building a slightly less domestic character. 50mm thick hardwood bridge timbers form the floor; these also insulate the brick barrel-vaulted cellar below.

Broad horizontal industrial louvres echo the 'oversized' weatherboards and allow generous views and ventilation on three sides, to the north, south and east. The main opening in the west provides a dramatic raked portico for timber and wine deliveries. Two courtyards below the building's east face provide a perfect retreat for wine tasting after a day of experimentation with high-precision timber technology.

Below Ecoply's giant weatherboards contribute relevance and an individual expression.

Opposite Fine roof detailing where edges feather is a Mainwaring trademark. Upstairs workshop, downstairs cellar.

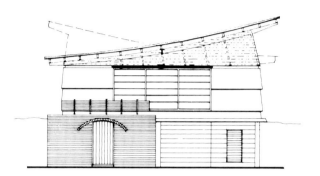

Below and right Industrial
louvres used in north, east
and west walls contribute to
high comfort levels and an
opening of vistas.

Opposite A high-tech
workshop illuminated with
low-tech common sense.

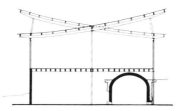

The identity of place

"Today, the challenge is to understand the richness of our cultural heritage and how it can contribute to new buildings and places of lasting value."

Lindsay and Kerry Clare

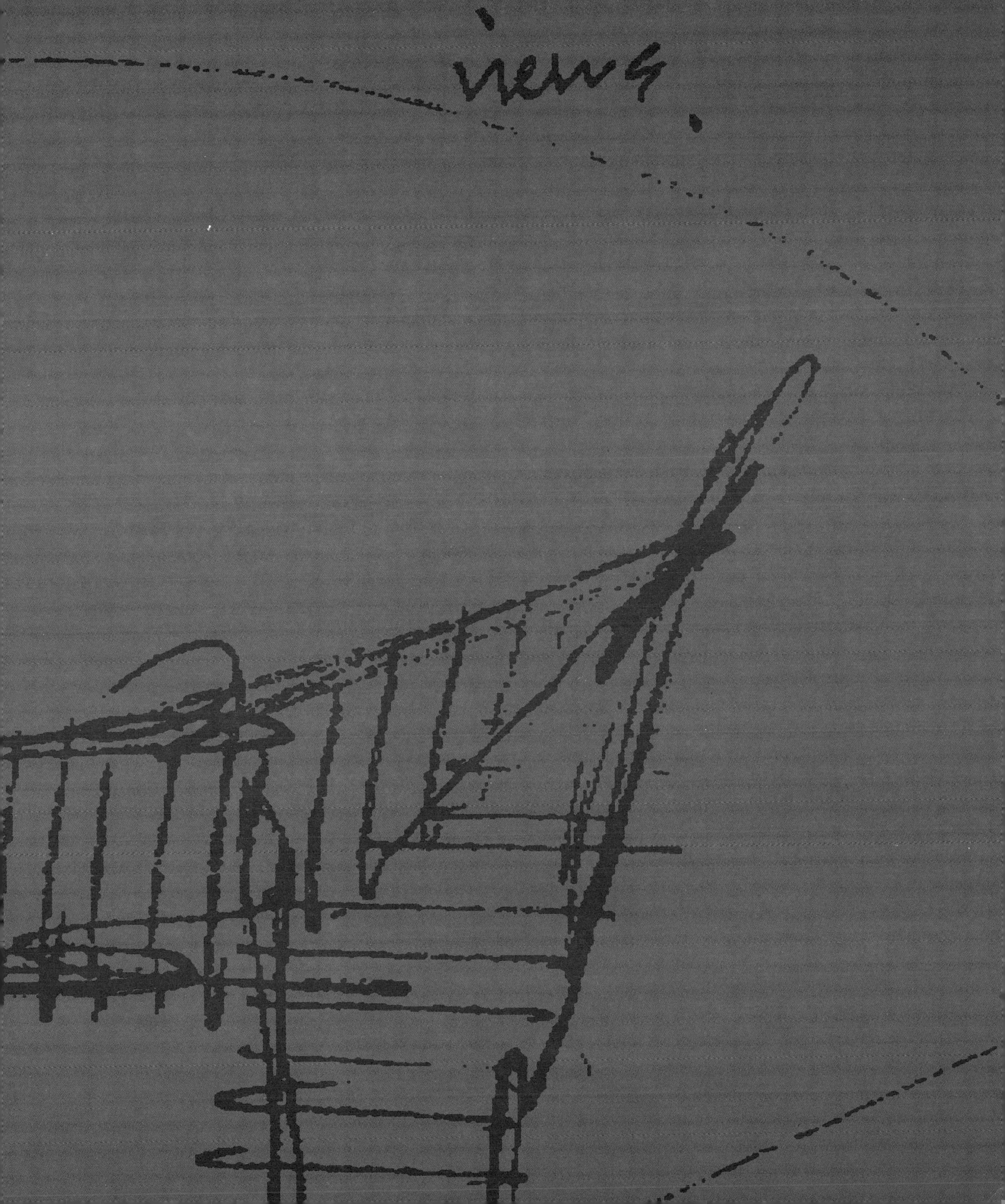
views

Our work sets out to create responsive architecture — an architecture that expresses the forces that shape it. Our work respects earth and light, relates to tradition and history, and acknowledges art as inseparable from life. We have developed a unique response to this culture and landscape that mediates change and technology without becoming sentimental or provincial. Our work is one piece in the mosaic that is Australia's identity.

Our work is often referred to as 'regional'; however, it is evident that when universal ideas or themes are accepted into a community, they are often selected, modified and moulded to become regional. What is relevant is that the work has developed as a design philosophy and process, not as a design style. This is important because it allows the work to respond to new content and experiences and therefore to move forward. In 1932, Van Loghem observed: 'Style was the by-product of getting a great number of quite other issues right. It was a reward; it could never be a starting point' (St John Wilson, 1995, p. 28).

Over the past few decades, many south-east Queensland architects have investigated alternative ways of living and this has led to new spatial arrangements and construction methods appropriate for a subtropical climate. The particularities of circumstance provide further opportunity for a varied response to cultural and environmental imperatives. Our own backgrounds, training and experience in the region have developed our awareness of nature, climate, geography, materials, skills and cultural patterns. Our architecture has become an expression of both attitude and circumstance.

Above
Porcellini Residence,
Flaxton, Noosa Hinterland,
(1996). An evocation of fine
layers and delicate strength.

Within this work we have focused on identifying fundamental values. In architecture, observing traditional methods and techniques reveals many essential qualities, such as the interactive relationship between building and people, context and environment. Local knowledge, common sense, intuition and dialogue are necessary to determine what is relevant and part of a continuous development. Our prime motivation is the quality of habitation.

The vast majority of our buildings draw on the lessons learned from traditional Queensland buildings that represent a synergy of building process and design. Our documentation process is another aspect that is a product of our region — primarily an inventiveness generated from necessity. The spare budget in the majority of commissions leaves no option but to ensure that there is a concentration of what is essential. This is also reflected in the built form in that the art of architecture becomes intrinsic to the tectonics. With many of these projects, if the art is not inseparable from the construction, it will probably be removed as a cost saving.

The most enjoyable clients are those who openly accept alternative solutions and have confidence in their own instincts rather than following the lead set by their neighbours. They prefer a lifestyle and environment that enriches the spirit. Many of our clients share our affinity in regard to life (and its imperfections), environment, art and community, and reject material pursuits. Today, the challenge is to understand the richness of our cultural heritage and how it can contribute to new buildings and places of lasting value. By addressing issues of culture, climate and landscape, architecture can become particular to place and yet expressive of a latent and emerging character.

Below Balanced daylight to interiors is a fundamental quality irrespective of building type or location.

Opposite top Slatted sunlight mediates inside and outside.

Opposite A transitional zone of louvres and screens. Sunroom of residence at Hamilton, Brisbane.

"Our work is often referred
to as 'regional'; however,
it is evident that when universal
ideas or themes are accepted
into a community, they are
often selected, modified and
moulded to become regional.
What is relevant is that
the work has developed
as a design philosophy
and process,
not as a design style."

Lindsay and Kerry Clare

Thrupp and Summers Residence
Nambour 1987

The site for the Thrupp and Summers residence is in the foothills of the Sunshine Coast hinterland. A ridge, chosen as the house site, is flanked by a large slope to the south and a small slope to the north. The land is well covered with eucalyptus that provides a dappled shade. Few trees were removed for construction and, at the clients' specific request, there was minimal site disturbance.

The planning encompasses climate control while resolving the clients' special requirements for a variety of activities. The large, open-plan living spaces and bedrooms are positioned to the north of a central gallery, with service spaces generally to the south. The client expressed a need for casual but minimalist interiors with a strong relationship to the landscape. An outdoor screened living area positioned at the north-west corner of the building makes an easy transition from the internal areas to the open deck which captures light, sun and a view of the ocean.

Large, open plan living spaces and bedrooms are positioned to the north of a central gallery, with service spaces generally to the south. A clerestory skylight over the gallery provides a balance of light to the interiors, as well as excellent ventilation. Further air flow is encouraged through the full-height louvres to the north and north-east. These areas of glass have provision for shading by external venetian blinds, but their installation is dependent on the extent of tree cover and growth. The eucalypts provide close to perfect sunshading. Summer sun does not penetrate the house, autumn/spring sunlight is filtered, and winter sunlight rakes past the tree trunks.

External materials of block, plywood and corrugated iron were chosen for their low-maintenance properties and aesthetic qualities. The combination of materials and colours produces a house of restraint and understatement in its Arcadian rural setting.

Above
Even minimal ground elevation contributes to improved thermal characteristics in the tradition of nineteenth-century 'Queenslander' stilt construction.

Opposite top Entry steps and building materials reflect lightweight spirit.

Below North elevation shows minimal overhang on heavily treed site.

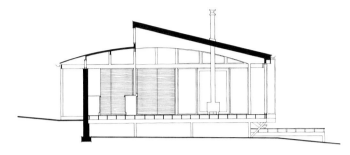

Below Interior of living area looking north-west to fly-screened verandah.

McWilliam Residence
Alexandra Headland 1990

Our clients had owned and holidayed in the original old timber beach shack on this site over a period spanning thirty years. Over this time the old house had gradually lost its views and been 'built out' by neighbours. The McWilliams decided to rebuild and create a dwelling platform high enough to regain lost views.

The accommodation requirements for the occupants on the upper level exceeded the areas required for guests and cars at the lower levels. The resultant platform structure was propped and strutted from below to dramatically dominate the building and float over the landscape, obtaining superb views.

In contrast to its exterior personality, the internal spaces are unprepossessing and modest. The plan revolves around a central masonry stairwell which functions as entry, breezeway and lightwell. The stairwell draws light into the centre of the plan on three levels.

Light and breeze to the stairwell space is balanced and controlled by a combination of a glazed southern wall at the entry level, glass bricks to the north at the mid level, and skylight glazing to the east and north on the upper level. Winter morning sun enters the skylight and penetrates beyond the stairwell, allowing light and warmth to reach secondary spaces aligning the western boundary.

Living spaces step around the stairwell, capturing views of the Pacific Ocean to the east, Noosa Heads to the north and the Blackall Ranges to the west. Framed views are also obtained to the south to Caloundra and the Glasshouse Mountains through carefully positioned openings within the enclosure of the southern wall.

Because of the tightness of the site and proximity of the neighbours, walls to the south and west are treated as a screening device using vertical batten treatments which are angled for privacy or sun protection.

Adjustable metal blade pergola roofs will be installed, providing two external living spaces to both the north and east sections of the deck. These areas of the deck also develop a sense of enclosure and containment by the use of a slatted balustrade which serves to frame and contain views from within. The open northern-eastern section of deck cantilevers out from the platform structure accentuating the drama of the view. The balustrade to this area is angled in for safety and constructed of flat metal and stainless steel wires, allowing the full impact of the view to the interiors.

The use of simple skillion roof forms was considered appropriate as a derivation of the traditional beach shacks found in the immediate area. The spaces created by the gentle roof slopes add intimacy to the casual and open feel of the plan.

Masonry walls inside and out are limewashed to provide a durable surface and to further develop a sunbleached palette of colours. Timbers are stained with oil-based stains which will also develop a washed and aged appearance.

Right The northern elevation has been 'in-filled' on the ground floor with an additional bedroom and ensuite.

Opposite A design that rises as an exuberant projection of platforms in search of ocean vistas.

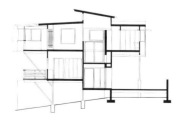

Left A Scandinavian aesthetic is evident in simple detailing treatments such as blond, battened timbers.

Below Screens and handrailing details contribute to a pervasive fineness of edge.

Opposite The pergola facilitates shade during summer, while slatted balustrades frame and contain views.

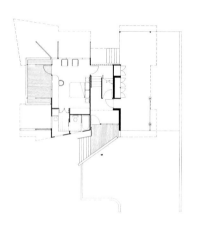

Rainbow Shores 'Surfside'
Rainbow Beach 1991

Rainbow Beach is a significant coastal site in that it lies between Fraser Island to the north and Cooloola National Park to the south. In addition to its coastal significance, the site is framed inland by the regional country towns of Gympie and Maryborough and the waters and community of Tin Can Bay. These towns are rich in character and possess many historic public and residential buildings, as well as demonstrating traditional self-generating town plan forms.

The site for Rainbow Shores had been previously cleared as a result of sand-mining activities. This development is the first stage of what will become a small town and it was essential to create the strong feeling of a distinct coastal community. Initial planning was based on creating a comprehensible neighbourhood with a density of approximately fifty dwellings per hectare. Combined pedestrian/vehicular traffic-circulation, and climatic and ecological concerns, set the planning framework.

A strong sense of order was used in the initial design concept to create and contain space in and around buildings. A comfortable disorder was introduced in response to issues such as landform and existing landscape, and through the specific identity of areas and spaces. Lightweight building materials such as bleached timber decking, painted fibre cement sheeting and stained plywood panels typical of the traditional 'Queenslander' contribute to the project's spirit and function.

Considerable time was spent on the site identifying trees, working with contours and plotting an access road to the buildings. Final building locations create a series of places or destinations within the street pattern. Variation in street width creates squares and parking courts. Curved and narrowed sections slow motor vehicles, while pedestrian use is encouraged to create friendly interaction and activity.

Breezeways within the building plans and sections allow cool air to circulate fully throughout the courtyard and interior spaces. While the buildings generally have a north-easterly aspect, in hot weather cooling breezes can also come from the south-east. We considered it appropriate that the architectural language should draw upon both the rich architectural resources in the Gympie and Maryborough area and the early, simply constructed, beach houses of the Sunshine Coast region.

Right Site plan — working around existing landform and trees.

Below Building above the tree tops captures cooling ocean breezes.

Opposite Town houses step to the north and east to gain ocean views.

184 Lindsay and Kerry Clare The Identity of Place

Opposite Streetscape
designed as a shared
pedestrian zone.

Below Ground-level plan
for one- and two-bedroom
units. First-level plan for
one- and two-level units.

Clare Residence Buderim 1991

This speculative house provides a model for a low-cost alternative to the fully tailor-made house. It is the first in a series of designs created to provide flexible yet affordable architecture. To achieve low construction costs, the structure was conceived as a two-storey timber box, framed and braced by plywood 'fin' walls along the perimeter. These fins also form alcoves along the perimeter that create useful areas for entry, storage or work space. No internal walls are required for bracing or load bearing. This allows a high degree of flexibility to the interior spaces and the placement of services.

The house has been sited across the contours to allow the full-width spaces to take maximum advantage of the landscape, sea views and the north-east aspect. The lower level comprises open-plan living areas, with the staircase and bathroom placed to create a separate bedroom/study space. Children's bedrooms and play areas are provided on the upper level in contained loft-like spaces.

Corrugated sheet steel used for external cladding has been scaled by deep louvre window recesses within the wall and by a continuous band of glazing to the upper floor. The street elevation utilises a combination of metal louvres and battened eave struts to maintain sun control, privacy and breeze penetration. The north-east elevation is quite private, allowing the house to open to the views and the land with glass louvres and swing doors.

Internally, the expression of the portal system provides a cohesive order throughout the length of the building, although the five bays vary in width according to the program. The experience of the space created is a strong combination of both the tectonic and tactile — for example, the living, dining and kitchen spaces are combined, yet are delineated by a number of devices. Fin walls, together with the colour and expression of beams — floor insets of hoop pine — reflect beam positions and the platform step. Plywood stairs, timber screen and built-in ply furniture blur the living room edge, yet give definition to spaces that are simultaneously drawn together by the ceiling and wall planes, materials and colours.

Fibre cement sheeting allowed flexibility and, once painted, are brightly coloured east and west walls to contrast the corrugated metal sheeting. Plywood is used extensively as a structural element to brace walls and ceiling planes, as well as providing an attractive, workable internal lining.

The vertical connection between both floor levels, achieved by voids and an open stair, fundamentally allows air movement and a balance of natural light to the interior spaces. The voids have a second function, which is to allow more community rather than separateness for the occupants. For our own family we wanted to engender a cooperative attitude with the relationships of spaces and the hierarchy of zones, without denying suitable amounts of privacy.

The house has been conceived as a loose-fit skeletal structure that can be clad and subdivided according to site, program and material preference. The concept allows potential to adapt the house to suit individual needs and to offer flexibility for the changing requirements of a family.

Above The building steps out over the gully to the west.

Below East elevation articulates a simple, fibre cement wall. Note the sculptural treatment of water collection.

Opposite The house is sited across contours to allow full-width spaces to take maximum advantage of the landscape, sea views and north-east aspect.

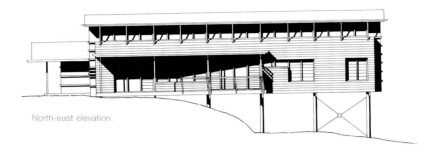

North-east elevation.

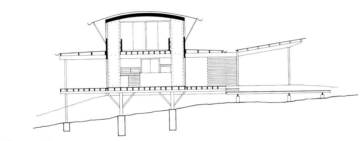

Cross section.

South-west elevation.

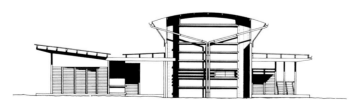

South-east elevation.

Right top Living room
looking east.

Right middle Family room
looking east. Note plywood
columns which frame
and brace the box structure.
As for ventilation,
light and interaction run
other side. Painting by
the children.

Right below Dining room
looking west.

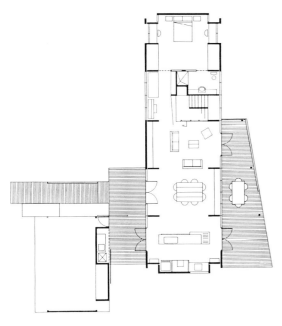

Ground-floor plan.

Ski 'n' *Skurf* Cable Ski Kiosk Bli Bli 1994

Even a remarkably beautiful region such as the Sunshine Coast can be reduced to 'placelessness' and kitsch at the hands of the tourist industry. Many people regret the loss of authenticity that pervades not only tourist facilities but also shopping centres, public places, streetscapes and housing within the region.

Ski 'n' *Skurf* tourist park caters for the young 'surfie' set. Waterskiing can be experienced without the need for a boat. The building serves the surf culture and is enriched (in its acknowledgment of water, sun, youth and sport) rather than reduced by it.

Only some 5 kilometres from the ocean and located close to a slow bend in the Maroochy River, the ski complex relates closely to its low-lying caneland environment. On visiting the complex, visitors hopefully experience more than a ski ride. Rather than a typically superficial, or partial, experience of theme parks, the visitor is met with a genuine building that expresses both new content and excitement without losing relation to its place.

A new kiosk/pavilion was to be fully designed, documented and approved by council and built within sixteen weeks in readiness for the Christmas tourist season. The excitement and energy of such a tight program is reflected in the end product. The experience of drawing details in the morning, delivering on site by lunchtime and seeing them built by the next day was extremely invigorating. This celebratory feeling is encapsulated within the building. It is a culture house of casual, vibrant and flexible spaces under gentle roof forms. Many of the groups that frequent the building arrive for breakfast, spend the day, and then take advantage of night skiing and a restaurant and bar that operate in summer.

The building is placed on a narrow spit of land between two lakes and was built on the original timber piles that survived a fire. These ready foundations set the site and building position. As the new building bears no resemblance to the original kiosk, there are some interesting spans and cantilevers to be discovered from below. For speed of construction and flexibility of use, the building was designed as a simple portal frame shed structure with surrounding ancillary amenities and verandah spaces.

Timber posts were bolted to existing piles, creating a platform over which the main structures were placed. Materials such as plywood and fibre cement sheet were chosen for lightness, durability and economy. The combination of simple planning, structural expression and robust finishes creates a suitably light, informal building inextricably of the Sunshine Coast.

Opposite View from south-east across ski lake showing cable pulley system.

North elevation.

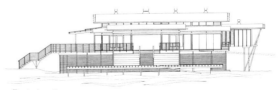

East elevation.

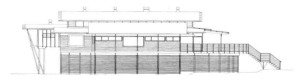

West elevation.

South elevation.

Right Amenities wing
stepping over the 'fast'
northern lake for water
skiers and 'boarders'.

Above Entry ramp and
western lake. A 'beach'
kiosk with attitude. Designed
primarily for teenagers and
young adults, the project's
use of appropriate materials
helps it to successfully
convey a suitable informality.

Opposite Lightweight
timber frame and plywood
panels contributed to a
sixteen-week turnaround
for the project.

Hammond Residence Cooran 1994

The Hammond residence is a product of humble aspirations. It has a simplicity and reduction that belies its strength and independence. The compact plan and economy of materials has resulted in an unmistakably rural expression. Charles and Cheryl Hammond retired from Townsville where they had lived in a traditional 'Queenslander'. They had lived in the New Guinea highlands and knew the importance of building for climatic conditions.

In contrast to the vast surrounding landscape, this dwelling is reduced to simple elements and is modest in scale, form and budget. It enjoys a panorama that takes in the Sunshine Coast and the Pacific Ocean from south to north. The house is placed to take maximum advantage of aspect while carefully acknowledging both the climatic conditions and the rural setting. The site is within Queensland's cyclone region and the building is designed for a wind speed of 60 metres per second.

Due to its remote location, the house was planned to utilise as many prefabricated and pre-cut components as possible. This remoteness also forced the house to be self-sufficient, which suited the clients' wishes to minimise energy consumption and to employ basic ecological design principles. The reduction of energy and resource consumption together with the use of largely plantation timbers demonstrates that sustainable design strategies can be employed to substantial effect in small projects. Plywood facilitated some fabrication of exterior wall panels. 'Single-skin' walls make extensive use of plywood for bracing and cladding. The stud detail is especially effective and durable, as it eliminates the timber bottom plate which usually weathers badly on traditional Queensland houses.

While the house draws on the construction of traditional Queensland houses, it represents a synergy of building process and design which has a relevance and wider application in its low cost, planning and structural simplicity. Construction of this house is a further development and adaptation of the 'system' previously used in our own residence and demonstrates the flexibility embodied in the approach. The Hammonds describe the house as constantly revealing new moods and experiences. They delight, they tell us, 'in the ever-changing and redefining of spaces, imagery, materials and light'.

Below View from the south-east.

Right Lightweight, prefabricated construction materials express the structural systems approach for ecologically sustainable design.

Opposite top View from the west reveals the relationship of the house to its dramatic site.

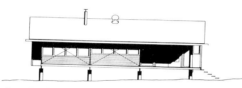

East elevation.

Cross-section.

North elevation.

Above Living area reveals
a debt to Scandinavian
design with battened
timber screens and
moulded ply furniture.

Opposite Living area/
study looking south
to Blackall Ranges.

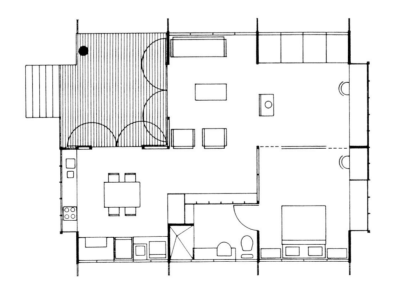

Pilot Housing Project Cotton Tree 1995

In 1992, three forums were held on the Sunshine Coast with representatives from government, development, professional and community sectors to investigate the provision of affordable housing that was socially, environmentally and aesthetically appropriate to the Sunshine Coast region. To help achieve these objectives, government cooperation was sought to free up planning processes and input was received from the community and end users.

The Cotton Tree Pilot Project was then undertaken with the support of the Sunshine Coast Regional Housing Council. Our commission came from the owners of adjoining sites — the Department of Public Works and Housing and the Beecham family. The land was considered an ideal siting for a pilot project, due to its strategic positioning with regard to public facilities, shopping and recreational areas.

The average household size on the Sunshine Coast is two people. One out of four households receives one or more forms of government financial assistance. Armed with such information from the Regional Housing Council's research, John Byrne, head of the State Government Special Projects, sought to achieve equitable housing that also provided an enriched lifestyle for occupants.

A study of changing demographics highlighted the inadequacies of the housing market in meeting community demands for more flexible and sustainable dwelling types. With the Cotton Tree project, there has been an attempt to provide housing for a mixture of family and single-occupant situations which has resulted in the provision of four three-bedroom family units (with ground access), one unit at ground level suitable for a disabled person and a series of bedsitter arrangements. Interestingly, the owners of the adjoining site (the Beecham family) wanted to build eight units all of which would be owned by different family members. In catering for the needs of the extended family, a housing mix similar to public housing resulted.

The retention of an existing stand of paperbark trees was achieved by the cooperative alteration and re-subdivision of shared boundaries. Planning, spatial and elevation approaches reinterpreted the traditional beach house types found in the area. The design consists of a series of attached and detached dwellings stepping from one storey to three storeys to facilitate solar access and catchment of sea breezes. As such, it provides an alternative and flexible model for higher density subtropical housing in older suburban and urban areas.

Below Existing paper bark trees were treated as crucial elements despite the pressure for higher density. Eastern view of two-storey town house.

Opposite South-western view of public housing adjacent to commercial zone on opposite side of the street.

North elevation (Public Housing).

South elevation (Public Housing).

Left Eastern view of town houses from community 'street'.

Below Although modestly priced, design principles are consistent throughout. Thus the stair and vertical breezeway promote a heightened spatial connection.

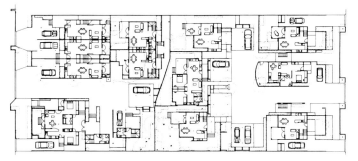

Ground floor private and public housing.

Porcellini Residence
Flaxton, Noosa Hinterland 1996

The Porcellinis' brief was to create, within a strictly limited budget and on a beautiful, elevated rural site, a sensitive yet simple house that was connected with the land. It was their idea to make the whole of the land their dwelling by the careful placement of a pavilion within the landscape.

The land falls to the south by locating a long thin pavilion at almost the midpoint of the site, leading to the creation of two outdoor 'rooms'. The linearly arranged rooms all connect directly to a small northern yard, reducing the need for and expense of a built verandah. A small cut in the land provides undercover car accommodation and storage, as well as entry by the southern stair. The southern entry and deck responds both to the view and the desire for privacy to the northern spaces and yard. Planting along the northern boundary will reinforce privacy to the north.

In section the house has been carefully considered with regard to view, climate and sense of containment. The scale of the simple roof has been moderated by providing a low, flat roof along the long northern edge. This section promotes the exhaust of hot air during summer months and allows deep penetration of winter sunlight. The scale creates a balance between the immediate view of the northern landscape and broader views of the Kondalilla National Park to the south. The ordered plan and staggered section, combined with the placement in the slope, make a fluid link with the landscape.

Right The rural pavilion. An exquisitely simple concept installed gently on the landscape. View from the north overlooking the Kondalilla National Park.

Opposite below Living space looking east illustrates the narrow waist of the lightly enclosed verandah.

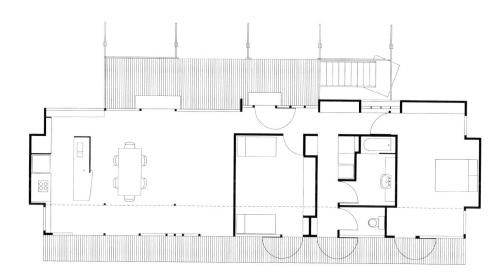

Below right The house protects to the north and projects to the south with large decks and parking underneath.

Opposite top Northern light splinters into the kitchen.

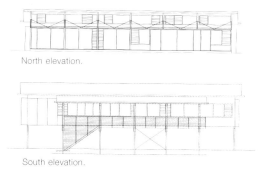

North elevation.

South elevation.

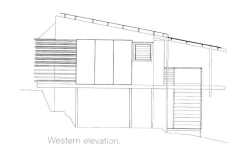

Western elevation.

University of the Sunshine Coast Recreation Building Sippy Downs 1997

Due to its location and function, the student club was able to be a less formal building than others on campus. The requirements for economy, flexibility, provision for future expansion, and a speedy design and construction (sixteen weeks in total), meant that the design had to be direct and robust. Within these parameters, we set out to embody the strength of the landscape, the quality of the light and the culture of the users.

The site was determined by the layout of playing sportsfields and straddles one of the drainage swales which separates the two fields along a north–south axis. The building was obliged to follow this axis and this results in its linear east and west facades opening out to view the sporting activity. This orientation was the generating criterion for what is essentially a very rational building.

The architectural solution results from an exploration of an appropriate section that could resolve the environmentally inefficient orientation and provide uninterrupted views to the fields. To optimise the views, load bearing and bracing are centralised through a series of posts and trusses. The plan is stepped to create a large north-east viewing deck. In section the building has been developed to work cross-ventilation and achieve balanced illumination. The stepped roof forms and east–west verandahs combine to reduce heat load and glare. In addition, this thinness of edge endorses the louvred glass fins and sliding glass doors. Plywood is used extensively to reinforce the link with John Mainwaring and Lawrence Nield's nearby USC library, as well as reinforcing its suitability as a material for public building.

Internally, the twin cantilevered columns support longitudinal box-ply trusses. In turn, this produces a top-lit colonnade which allows the central volume to be drenched in natural light, thus balancing the reflected light admitted via wall glazing.

Opposite left West elevation accentuates extended hat 'brim'.

Opposite Sleek, linear and vigorously animated, the amenities block sustains the design spirit.

Below An extroverted solution that extends the traditional verandah as a welcoming stage for student study and social events. The traditional verandah dematerialised heightens structural legibility.

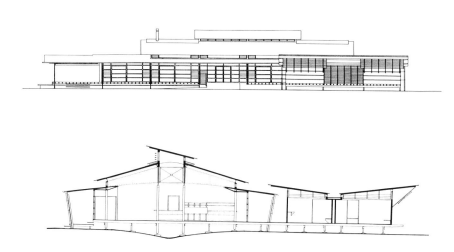

Opposite Resembling
an inverted boat hull
with plywood braced fins,
a top-lit colonnade
introduces additional light.

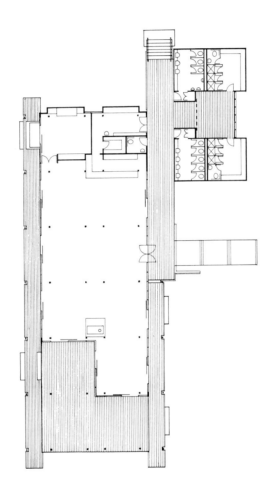

Residence at Hamilton Brisbane 1997

We had worked with these clients on a small commercial project on the Sunshine Coast in the 1980s. They owned a Gabriel Poole house, which they loved because it was simply planned around a large deck enclosed by insect mesh which allowed the internal spaces to casually connect with the outdoors. When we were asked to design a house in the established Brisbane suburb of Hamilton, their brief was for a house that captured the informal, relaxed style of their coastal house, within the constraints of a city house.

Requirements were for a large home on a small, constricted site that fell steeply to the south. Expansive southern views of the city and Brisbane River became the focus of the site. This conflicted with the desirable northern aspect that brings essential cooling breezes and warm sun in summer. The problem of orientation was resolved in section more than by plan.

By placing sleeping and living areas on three levels that are connected by a northern courtyard, winter sun and southern views are experienced from all of these spaces. A lap pool is the focus of this northern courtyard, providing a cooling backdrop and visual connection to the interiors. The section also creates a balance of light and draws summer breezes through all of the 'thin plan' levels. A triangular skylight pulls blue sky and winter sun deep into the plan and extracts hot air in summer.

The building is essentially concrete-framed, with cantilevered floor slabs extending beyond the masonry base to enable a finer, lighter expression. Lightweight battened plywood cladding on upper levels, a gently curved roof and fine sunshading elements allow the house to sit comfortably among the light, timber-framed historic houses of the suburb.

Interior finishes of blackbutt timber floors, silver ash cabinet work and western red cedar louvres combine with a rich colour scheme to create a city house for a subtropical climate. The project resolves a series of complex requirements on a demanding site in a simple, understated manner.

Right and below
Bay windows project from bedrooms along the northern elevation.

Opposite The lap pool and courtyard make a direct visual connection to central living spaces.

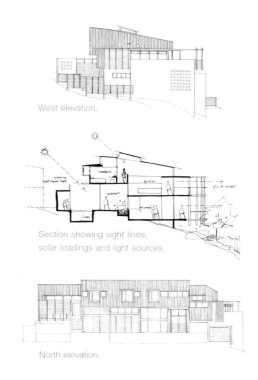

West elevation.

Section showing sight lines, solar loadings and light sources.

North elevation.

ft and below Living room
ins northern light from
light and pool terrace.

low right Dramatic skylight
ometry above bedroom
ssageway and living areas.

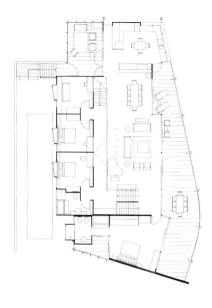

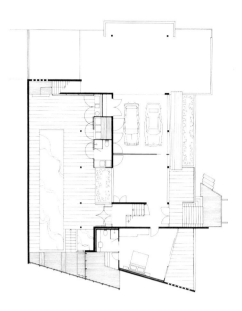

Selected bibliography